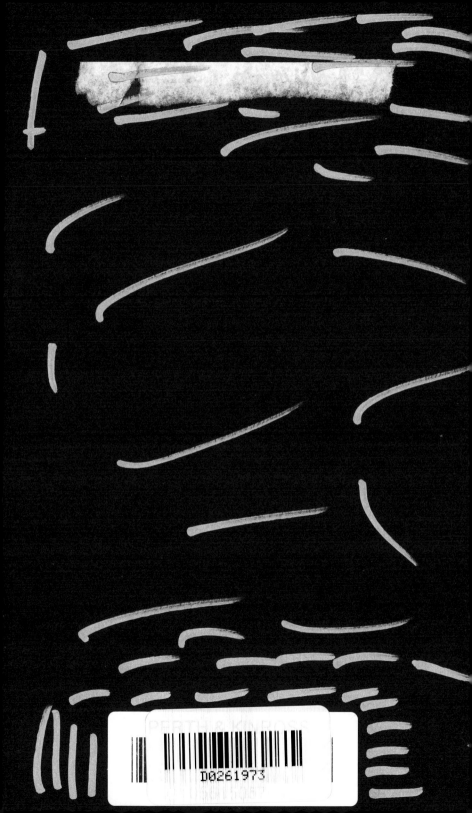

D0261973

BREAKFAST WITH SOCRATES

BREAKFAST WITH SOCRATES

The Philosophy of Everyday Life

Robert Rowland Smith

P

PROFILE BOOKS

First published in Great Britain in 2009 by
PROFILE BOOKS LTD
3A Exmouth House
Pine Street
London ECIR OJH
www.profilebooks.com

1 3 5 7 9 10 8 6 4 2

Typeset in Jenson by MacGuru Ltd
info@macguru.org.uk
Printed and bound in Great Britain by
Clays, Bungay, Suffolk

A CIP catalogue record for this book is available from the British Library.

ISBN 978 1 84668 237 7
eISBN 978 1 84765 208 9

The paper this book is printed on is certified by the © 1996 Forest Stewardship
Council A.C. (FSC). It is ancient-forest friendly. The printer holds FSC chain
of custody SGS-COC-2061

FSC
Mixed Sources
Product group from well-managed
forests and other controlled sources
Cert no. SGS-COC-2061
www.fsc.org
© 1996 Forest Stewardship Council

To my wife, Clare: she's always keen to make sure I eat breakfast, and this book is for her.

Contents

Acknowledgements   xi

Introduction   1
1 Waking up   4
2 Getting ready   14
3 Travelling to work   24
4 Being at work   32
5 Going to the doctor   43
6 Having lunch with your parents   54
7 Bunking off   63
8 Shopping   73
9 Booking a holiday   82
10 Going to the gym   91
11 Taking a bath   100
12 Reading a book   108
13 Watching TV   119
14 Cooking and eating dinner   128
15 Going to a party   138
16 Arguing with your partner   147
17 Having sex   157
18 Falling asleep and dreaming   166
Afterword   177

Further reading   180
Index   182

'How we spend our days is, of course, how we spend our lives.'

Annie Dillard, *The Writing Life*

Acknowledgements

I OWE THANKS to many people who've supported, challenged and inspired me in the writing of this book. First among these is Richard Vine, who was my original sounding board, continued to offer great advice, and came up with the title (later on I was to discover a poem of the same name by Constantine Cavafy). I'd also like to pick out James Fulton for his constant interest and encouragement, and my co-religionists at the School of Life – Sophie Howarth, of course, as well as Caroline Brimmer, Angharad Davies, Mark Vernon and Harriet Warden; people at the BBC who've shown such interest – Susanne Curran, Eliane Glaser, Anne Mensah, Andrea Miller, Rebecca Stratford and Matthew Sweet; David Edmunds and Nigel Warburton, the pair behind *Philosophy Bites*; not to mention Judith Hemming, and the many stars who constellate around her, who helped unlock the systemic energy necessary for such an endeavour; the same goes for Mother Meera. No less important in different ways were Eileen Acebey, Emily Browning, John Bruce-Jones, Cathie Clearwater, Katrina Coulson, Peter Cox, Lynn Fabes, Ian Fletcher, Andrew Foster, Beatrice Fraenkel, Moira Gibb, Matthew Herbert, Victoria Hobbs, Andrew Jackson, Neil Litherland, Anthony Mellors, Anna Mike, Kate and Ben Munn, Paul Myerscough, Martin Newman, Sophia Parker, Julia Pritchett, Frank Romany, Steve Rose, Polly Russell, Rupert Symons, Sophie Taylor, Roger Thornham, Adam Wishart and Andrea Wulf.

The book would not have got off the ground, however, without two particularly talented individuals: my excellent agent, Stephanie

Ebdon, whose careful tenacity and natural wit have helped this book to make an impression around the world already; and my editor at Profile Books, Daniel Crewe, whose exceptional mixture of human warmth and editorial coolness has made working with him a pleasure and an education. I would also like to acknowledge the people who've supported Steph and Daniel in turn: at the Marsh Agency, Annina Meyerhans, Caroline Hardman, Camilla Ferrier and the late Paul Marsh himself; and at Profile, Ruth Killick, Penny Daniel and Andrew Franklin. Hilary Redmon at the Free Press in New York and Lesley Levene also played a valuable part. Together, they're pretty much the dream team.

Finally, my love and thanks to my daughters, Zoë, Esther and Eden.

Introduction

GIVEN THAT SOCRATES was assassinated by poison, you might think twice before accepting his invitation to breakfast. Yet what got him killed is exactly what would make him an excellent breakfast companion – his curiosity. He was silenced for asking too many questions, getting up too many people's noses. His mind was probing, dissatisfied, inventive, and it led him to bring everything, from the purpose of the law to the origin of sex, into doubt – no wonder his most famous pupil, Plato, characterised him as an irritating insect. Were you actually to sit down with him for cappuccino and croissants, he might start by asking why you lead the life you lead, or what value you have as a person. It's a style that might cause you, like the state that had him murdered, to take offence; but, on the other hand, were you to give him the benefit of the doubt, you'd be taken on an extraordinary mental journey. He might explain why genius and madness are so closely linked, or how the universe is made up of the soul; on a more personal level, he might set out the reasons why being good is more important than being happy. Famously, Socrates declared, 'The unexamined life is not worth living', and, preferring dialogue to giving speeches, he'd get you to reflect on your self and your actions in a way that would either lend them greater meaning or inspire you to make changes, and so create the meaning that your life lacked.

Pretty much the same would apply if you were to have a bagel with Hegel or eggs with Bacon. Although there have been excruciating debates in philosophy about how many angels can stand on a pinhead and the difference between being and Being, its spirit is not to make up conundrums for boffins, but to help us pursue wisdom. After all, the word 'philosophy' means 'the love of wisdom', and being wise is not the same as being clever. Where cleverness satisfies itself with winning arguments in the abstract, wisdom is a practical art, aimed at making deft judgements in the midst of everyday complications. In this sense, philosophy is about recognising the ambiguity of life as it is lived, and Socrates would be just as interested in how much to tip the waiter for serving you the toast and muffins as in whether God exists.

This book tries to follow suit: it shows how history's greatest ideas – not just from philosophy, in fact, but psychology, sociology and politics – relate to how you live your life, and how you can be more thoughtful about it. True, there are plenty of in-depth works on this subject – on how to act ethically, what kind of political party you should vote for and so on. The difference is that, apart from being written in technical language, they tend to keep the big ideas aloft, rather than grounding them in everyday experience, which is the purpose of this book. The following pages, therefore, conjure up various geniuses who will accompany you while you go about your business. You're at the gym and the social historian Michel Foucault runs beside you to explain how your exercise routine is a form of state control. Jacques Lacan, a psychoanalyst, becomes your personal shopper and, as you gaze into the fitting-room mirror, lets you in on the perils of narcissism. While you're at work, Karl Marx whispers in your ear about how to stop being a wage slave. You'll encounter Mach- iavelli offering advice on throwing a successful party, hear from Carl Schmitt on why fighting with your partner might be a good thing, and learn tips from the Buddha on how to avoid falling asleep in the bath. As they apply themselves to thinking about your morning ritual, or what you watch on TV, you'll find out something about them. Their ideas might be challenging or bizarre, but always relevant to how you spend your day.

Of course, that day might not follow the pattern set out here. Not everyone has sex on a daily basis, and lunch with your parents might – thankfully, perhaps – be no more frequent than an annual event. If you work from home, then 'travelling to work' is unlikely to involve the travails described in Chapter 3, where I refer to Thomas Hobbes, the seventeenth-century political theorist, to explain why the morning commute brings out the savage in us. Equally, there'll be things omitted you might have wished to see, and an alternative version of this book might include 'Picking the kids up from school', 'Seeing your therapist', 'Going to Pray' or 'Working the nightshift'. But most of the experiences described here should be ones you recognise, and you will be equipped with tools to think about them afresh.

Not that it's all about 'big ideas' from big thinkers. Along with some thoughts of my own, you'll find references to music, painting, film, literature and even a remarkable Japanese experiment into water crystals. In 'Going to the doctor' you'll discover a serious study on pain, as well as the funniest joke in the world (allegedly). 'Cooking and eating dinner' brings in French anthropology alongside Peter Greenaway's film of culinary decadence, *The Cook, The Thief, His Wife and Her Lover*. I have used whatever material – old, new, borrowed or blue (the chapter on sex discusses pornography) – that might bring meaning to the mundane, humour to the humdrum, reason to the routine.

If it's true that the unexamined life is not worth living, instead of waiting for a lecture on the subject, why not examine it in the moment? After all, the everyday is 99 per cent of our lives – if we don't think about it while we live it, there's not going to be much time left over for reflection. And if we do, we might learn to appreciate the importance behind the apparently trivial things we do so automatically, like getting dressed or falling asleep, and see them in a new light.

Waking up

THERE IS A LOVELY SONG called 'Alive', by Mara Carlyle, that opens with the lines:

I'm surprised by the sun every day I wake up,
I'm surprised by waking up!

Mara's voice swings from woozy to perky as she sings, mimicking the change from slumber to consciousness. What's cute about the lyric is that it re-enacts the childlike wonder of waking up, the wonder that the world is still there, that the person waking still exists. Even for grown-ups, waking after too little sleep, or with a hangover, or beside the wrong lover, or following a series of troubled dreams, there is a moment, just before the jaundice or despair reloads, when simply to be awake again, and still alive, is an amazing surprise.

Why is that? Why, even though we do it every single day, can waking up still surprise us? Is it precisely because, until that moment, you were sleeping and therefore not alert enough to be able to predict that you were about to wake up? If that is so, then technically speaking waking up can't not be a surprise – because right before it you are, by definition, asleep.

So even though waking up might be the most foreseeable event in our lives, as dependable as the sun rising in the morning, we never actually see it coming. Predictable and unpredictable in equal measure, waking up is a paradox – a kink in the straight logic of things – which is just one of the reasons why it's worth thinking about. In fact, as ordinary as it seems, waking up is one of the profoundest actions we can take. It may sound odd to say that there is a philosophy of waking up, but in a way the whole of philosophy is about nothing else.

For hundreds of years, 'philosophy' has concerned itself with questions of consciousness, and being conscious, obviously enough, implies being awake. It's true that at the end of the nineteenth century we begin to get full-blown philosophies of *unconsciousness* – that's what psychoanalysis is all about – but far and away the dominant trend in philosophy has been to focus on conscious phenomena, on waking life – what it is to think, to feel, to know, to believe, to sense, to perceive, to act, to choose, to like, to love, to do good and to do evil: activities that all belong to the realm of waking rather than sleeping.

So there you are: you're awake. You may not be a morning person, but if you're awake, at least you're conscious. Or are you? How do you know you're not still asleep? How do you know you're not dreaming being awake? How do you know that everything around you, including yourself, is not an illusion, a trick played on you by some malevolent sprite?

This, of course, has become one of the most famous philosophical questions of all and the most famous philosophical answer to it came in the 1630s from René Descartes, a Frenchman who lived most of his life in the Netherlands. Like most philosophers confronted with a perplexing world, Descartes wanted to establish some certainties, and his conceit was to do so by turning philosophy on its head. Rather than starting with a hypothesis, or a set of assumptions, or a first principle, or a scientific law, he committed to start with nothing and to take nothing for granted: he would doubt absolutely everything, on a sort of 'guilty until proven innocent' basis, and see where it led him.

Applying this sceptical method, Descartes arrived imperturbably at the realisation that he could doubt everything except the fact that he was doubting. What's more, if he was doubting, he had to be thinking. He then realised that only something that exists can think – how can something be thought without someone to do the thinking? Descartes was inching towards a discovery. Putting two and two together, he concluded that if you can think, you must exist. For even if you think you're dead, the fact that you *think* you're dead means you're alive, because thinking implies existing. Descartes had found proof of existence. Hence his legendary epigram 'I think, therefore I am.' It was a giant leap forward not just for philosophy but for science in general, because it seemed to establish something irrefutable, and thereby provided solid ground for all further investigation.

This is why waking up in the morning is such a philosophical act, a direct encounter with consciousness and existence. Really it's ironic that we do it so unconsciously, because when we wake up we're not only returning to consciousness, we're also regaining the ability to prove it. During the night it wasn't so certain. Although dreaming is a kind of thinking, and so another way, in theory, of proving that you exist, there were whole stretches of the night when you weren't either thinking or dreaming, which raises the tricky question of whether you existed in those times: if thinking implies existing, do you exist when you're not thinking? It's a question I come back to in the last chapter of this book. For now, you know that you exist at least in the daytime.

So, having taken philosophy right back to square one, Descartes made this great jump forward, and as you stretch in the morning, no matter how grumpy you might be, you're embracing an invisible but extraordinary phenomenon – your own conscious existence, your own awareness that you're there. This seems like a promising start, but having hard-boiled things to this perfect egg of thought, from which everything else should have followed, Descartes was somewhat uncertain as to what to do with his certainty. You're now awake, you're conscious and you exist – but what next?

Being awake and conscious tends to be associated with having your faculties about you – where the word 'faculties' effectively means your ability to think coherently, to reason things out. But just because you're awake, does it automatically mean that your faculties of reason are working? It might not always feel like it – getting your brain into gear can take a little time – but as your eyes adjust to the light, is your reason waking up too? This is an important question, because you can be conscious and mad – being conscious and being rational don't always go together. And it would be quite good in the morning to know not just that you exist, but that you're thinking straight.

Let's say that as you swim up into consciousness through the bedclothes – doubting your existence, perhaps, but thereby proving it – you become aware of the traffic outside your window: perhaps a pneumatic drill decides to join the chorus, or the recycling truck comes by and the clash of broken glass keeps shattering the peace. You curse the noise and sink back into your pillow. Sitting at the end of your bed, Immanuel Kant, who was in his prime about 150 years after Descartes, would immediately challenge you – and not just because he was a renowned insomniac, famous for working all night in nightcap and robe. He'd certainly wonder if your reaction was rational. Why?

Watching you trying to retreat under the duvet, Kant would argue that your waking perception that the sound of traffic is noisy is nothing more than that – a perception. You're not necessarily making a rational judgement and your reason may indeed still be asleep. For how can you be sure the noise you hear is the true noise and not just a reflection of your grumpiness? Is your reaching again for the covers the action of what Kant called 'pure reason' – a universal truth that's out there for everyone – or is it a personal response of laziness and avoidance?

You might imagine that everywhere on your street people are cursing along with you, but even if you were to poll your neighbours, and they all agreed that the morning traffic on your street is indeed particularly irritating, still Kant wouldn't be satisfied. He'd be pushing not just for an empirical or democratic version of the truth, but for something more enduring – pure reason, again – which lies above, beyond and before any interpretations, individual or collective, that are made about reality. And if you think that in this Kant is being unre-alistic, or dogmatic, or unduly severe, you need only remind yourself of certain cults, where 100 per cent of the membership believe one thing to be true and 100 per cent of them are deluded. Universal belief in something doesn't equate to universal truth, and Kant was keen to refer back to Copernicus, the Polish polymath who in 1514 proved that the earth goes round the sun. Until that point, everybody believed the earth lay at the centre of the universe, and everybody was wrong.

It's clear that, apart from its many other uses – birth, death and the consummation of marriage, to name a few – the bed is a battleground for philosophies of waking up. Even if it provides firm support for the idea that you exist, it can't be trusted to bear the weight of your perceptions; and while waking up relieves you of a large degree of doubt (Descartes), it immediately replaces it with the task of proving that what you feel first thing in the morning has any substance at all (Kant). The day has barely begun and you've already had quite a philosophical workout, and yet if philosophy has pondered these questions at such length, it is probably not philosophy but religion, and Christianity in particular, that has most leveraged the idea of waking up. For apart from anything else, the act of waking up is a playing out in miniature of the relationship between life and death, where going to sleep is like dying and waking up is like being born or born again. That relationship is not just metaphorical, however: there's a very literal sense in which, when you go to bed, you can't guarantee that you will ever wake up again. On both counts, Christianity has a special relevance.

Consider this: there's not much point to Christianity without Christ, and there's not much point to Christ without the resurrection – his alleged rising from the grave three days after dying on a cross he'd been nailed to by Roman soldiers. Christianity, to put it baldly, is a religion of waking up. It is the conviction that, for all the mystery shrouding it, death is literally only a sleep; and that you will, if you play your cards right, wake up again afterwards in paradise. What is known grandly as 'resurrection' is an ordinary miracle, transcendent yet trivial, blessed but banal, as is brought out brilliantly in a wittily naïve painting of the same name by a British artist of the mid-twentieth century, Stanley Spencer. The painting depicts the folk of an English village getting out of their graves, in their nightclothes, stretching and yawning, as though they have simply woken up in bed. The painting does what Christianity does: it treats death as an unthreatening interlude, no more scary than turning in for the night. As long as you've said your prayers, you can look forward to waking up in heaven.

But, of course, if there is this emphasis in Christianity on reawakening, its job in part is to outstare the alternative, namely that when you go to bed you won't wake up at all. In this latter view, rather than death being like sleep which you'll wake up from, sleep threatens to become the death from which you'll never wake up again. It's interesting that one of Shakespeare's sonnets refers to sleep as 'death's second self', because at first sight it seems that Shakespeare is comparing sleep with death in a rather conventional metaphorical way; but on closer inspection, he's saying that sleep is not just *like* death, it's death's 'second self' – that is, it's a clone of death, or at best a dark emissary you would do well to treat with deference and trepidation. He takes the Christian idea that sleep and death are equivalent and throws it back at Christianity. Going to sleep is risky, he implies, because, rather than waking into the afterlife, you may well never wake up again – in the late 1590s, when Shakespeare was writing, average life expectancy was about thirty and the infant mortality rate was spectacularly higher than today.

Small wonder, then, that when you awake, even in the twenty-first century, and slip the embrace of this shadowy stranger called sleep, you might still feel, beneath the magical surprise, a modicum of relief and even gratitude. And if Christianity profits from the fear implied in that, there's another reason why the territory of waking up is so comfortably claimed by Christianity – and Islam too, for that matter. Although it's determined by bodily rhythms, waking up lies psychologically at the mercy of something, or someone, else. The fact that we have been asleep and unconscious means waking up involves the disquieting sense of it being out of our control – it happens to us rather than us making it happen – so that this moment of rescue that is the coming back into consciousness is easily attributed to divine intervention, as if an angel had snatched you back from the underworld.

Of course, the connotations of 'underworld' are more pagan than religious, but religion hasn't been averse to benefiting also from the emotive power of paganist ritual, even if officially it has sought to distance itself. After all, if you're hoping to get a new religion off the ground, you want to tap into as much of the symbolic repertoire available as you can — and then claim it was all your own. In any case, from its earliest beginnings, Christianity has harboured an occult strain which draws the link from the resurrection of Christ to the waking up of the earth in spring. We know, for example, that Easter assimilated an existing 'pagan' festival that celebrated the lengthening of the days with a 'rite of spring' or a 'song of the earth'. It's not so much that religion picked up where magic left off, converting the dark continent of superstition with the light of true belief — which tends to be how the story gets told — but rather that religion incorporated magic, assimilated or ingested it, drawing particular strength from its elemental focus on reawakening. All of which makes, of course, for a heady mix — the world groaning into wakefulness, the ice splitting, the tubers stirring, and the whole cosmic rhythm incorporated into a scene of priests solemnifying the return of the light of the world — and yet in our own small way, from our beds, we too reprise this supernatural motion of the natural year on a daily basis, simply by waking up.

The associations get only richer and more intense when you realise that the very concept of truth — the cornerstone of philosophy and religion alike, let alone the law — also rests heavily on the meaning of waking up. And you don't need to be a philosopher to appreciate it, because there are clues to its dependency in everyday phrases such as 'waking up to the truth', 'my eyes were opened' and even 'wake up and smell the coffee'. If such phrases hint that waking up and truth are bedfellows of some sort, you need only go back to the ancient Greek for corroboration. There you'll find that the word for truth is '*aletheia*', from which in English we get the word for 'lethargy'. But see how the Greek word is 'a-letheia' rather than 'letheia' — that is, truth is the *opposite* of lethargy. And what is the opposite of lethargy, if not waking up? The truth lies in being awake and throwing off the sheets. In a certain sense, you're most truly yourself when you awake – it's hard to wake up inauthentically.

The point is easy to miss, however. It's not just that you need to wake up if you're going to see or hear the truth, as important as that might be; rather, it's that the truth itself is nothing other than a kind of waking up. How does that work? Turning to a third philosopher, G. W. F. Hegel, will shed some light.

Hegel, a German philosopher of the early nineteenth century, writing shortly after Kant, was also interested in Christ's prodigious waking up after death, and not least because it demonstrated what Hegel called 'absolute truth'. According to the story, Christ passed through three phases: first he was alive, then he died and finally – if it's a story you believe – he was reborn. And unless he had been reborn – unless he had woken up again after death – he wouldn't have been Christ but a charlatan, not the true messiah but a fake. Jesus became Christ only at the third step, when the truth about him was revealed, confirmed and completed. What's more, he could have become himself *only* at the third step – take away that third step, or any of the preceding two, and he no longer makes sense as Christ. So the three-part structure was essential to the disclosure of his truth.

Extraordinary as he may be, in this respect Christ is an ordinary example of how truth must always obey this law of three steps, in which the final step is a waking up, a climactic becoming true. In fact, anything of consequence in Hegel works in threes – a mechanism he called the 'dialectic' – where the truth is a kind of cosmic alarm clock that brings the world to its senses after a period of activity followed by rest. The very course of history has followed the same pattern, according to Hegel, in its gradual unfolding. First came the ancient Greek phase, which was full of sweetness and light, and even contained in it the germ of truth, but remained too ideal and ungrounded. The Greeks thought they were awake, but they weren't. Then came the classical Roman phase, which was all too real and adult, but deadening by the same token – impressively important, granted, but terribly dry and judicial, as if putting things back to sleep through excessive ordering. At last the German phase arrives, the phase that Hegel himself was on the verge of witnessing, promising to blend the best of the Greek and the Roman but surpass them both, history's final expression or renaissance, the proper rebeginning of the meaning of the world. History, for Hegel, was to wake up to its truth in the German nineteenth century.

A bit later into that century, Hegel's theory was to inspire a whole new school of thought that included such important thinkers as Jacob Burckhardt, Eduard Winkelmann and Karl Marx, but to a modern ear, of course, Hegel's claim sounds all too pat and self-aggrandising. Does anyone seriously believe, in our relativist world, that there are any absolute truths left to be woken up? Apart from religious or polit-ical fundamentalists, almost certainly not – but it would be far easier to mock Hegel's interpretation of history if it hadn't, as the base nar-rative of Aryan destiny, provided grist to the Nazi mill – the hymning of 'Tomorrow Belongs to Me', so chillingly imagined in Bob Fosse's 1972 film *Cabaret*, is a way of announcing a renaissance or reawaken-ing of a destiny that has been put nefariously to sleep. Even in much less ominous terms, the idea that the truth is something that has been languishing and needs to be woken, dragged from its bed and brought into the light of day, maintains an instinctive appeal. Think, for example, of the political gesture favoured by conservatives of all stripes in all countries which involves reviving a truth that has been dormant, be it an exhortation to 'get back to basics' or the plea to 'return to core values'. The gesture is essentially Hegelian or dialectical, because it presumes that the truth was once there, then it was covered up or put to sleep (usually by the 'opposition'), and now it is incum-bent upon us to resuscitate it or wake it up again. The truth is all the more true, and all the more potent, if it is *reawoken*.

We're now two hundred years beyond Hegel, and whether we have finally woken up to the truth or still loll about in our 'dogmatic slum-bers' (as Kant once put it), we are asked to stay awake in a much more obvious way, a way that is a far cry from either philosophy or religion. For although you might rate the general level of consciousness in the world deplorably low, you'd have trouble denying that ours is a culture of wakefulness. You'd more than likely accept that we who live in capitalist societies, in cities that never sleep, inhabit the zone of the non-stop, of the 24/7, of round-the-clock surveillance and of being constantly vigilant. In real terms, it's increasingly hard to find the off switch, whether it belongs to our body or our BlackBerry. This means that, in so far as waking up implies having let ourselves fall asleep and take our eye off the screen, it's become less a part of the natural order of things and more a nostalgic luxury. Have we encroached upon an era in which the best we can hope for is not achieving proper sleep but remaining on standby?

If the answer is yes, it's almost certainly down to two intertwining imperatives – twin gods, really, that it's become practically heretical to doubt. They are economic growth and technological innovation: ever higher GDP and upgrades ad infinitum. Together they have forced a global productive insomnia whereby the moment Japan goes to sleep, America wakes up and hurries to the screen. No break in production is to be tolerated, for the world has been recast as a factory whose goal is output, whose mode is efficiency and in which 'waking up', if it suggests having been asleep, is for wimps.

What drives those twin gods in turn, generating this economic wakefulness, is not just money but morals. For all the vice it fosters in the form of overconsumption, such mechanical and monetary madness testifies to the eternal virtue of hard work. Don't forget that being awake and industrious stand now, and are likely to stand for ever, in higher regard than being asleep and lazy. We are living out the logic of what Max Weber dubbed the Protestant work ethic, which does a lot of good, but brings unintended consequences, and is an ethic that depends, at bottom, on getting up and getting going. The moment you wake up, you're drawn into it.

But, of course, between getting up and getting to work stands an important step.

2

Getting ready

DON'T THINK that when Cleopatra offers to give Antony, as he's preparing to fight, an 'armour of gold' that it's all terribly exotic, remote and extravagant. She's only doing what the stereotypical suburban housewife does when she packs her husband off to catch the ten past eight to London Bridge, Grand Central or Shinjuku Station.

Mark Antony may not work in the law, the media or the government, but the preparations he goes through are far less than a million miles away. It's not just that today we still apply martial metaphors to the most humdrum duties before us – 'going to do battle', 'facing the enemy' or, quoting the Bard directly, 'once more unto the breach' – it's because getting ready to go out calls for a war mentality every time.

It has to do with the yes-and-no nature of preparation. On the one hand, getting ready means adopting the frame of mind to experience something, to throw yourself into it, to submit to what lies ahead, to become embroiled, to take part and be present in events, and to follow the tide wherever it may take you: you are saying yes. But on the other hand, because getting ready means being prepared, you are also trying to do the opposite – to guard yourself against what might come at you, to limit your exposure, to head off potential surprises and keep your protective armour firmly strapped on: you are also saying no. As much as getting ready is about agreeing to dive into things in all their unpredictable glory ('Here goes nothing!'), it's also about holding the world at arm's length and keeping the experience *un*experienced ('I'm prepared for anything'). That is the paradox of getting ready: it's collecting yourself both to experience and not to experience the day ahead.

And while it is a paradox we encounter every day as we are packing our bag or putting on our jacket, it has deep philosophical roots that reach down at least as far as Mark Antony's first century BC, and it created a fissure of similar depth. On one side of it, you have those for whom the world is basically orderly and safe, safe enough for you to throw yourself into it. On the other, those who believe life to be much more a matter of chance, so you'd better buckle up – they'd argue that there wouldn't be a defensive aspect to getting ready to meet the world if the world itself didn't move in mysterious, and sometimes dangerous, ways.

Take one of Antony's Roman contemporaries, the philosopher Lucretius, who described this inscrutable energy of the world in a poem called 'On the Nature of Things'. The poem makes for an odd mix of psychology, physics and theology, and yet it's ahead of its time in that Lucretius argues that the cosmos is composed of millions of streaming atoms, and that the behaviour of these atoms is suscep-tible to random swings – almost as if he is describing Heisenberg's 'uncertainty principle' two thousand years *avant la lettre* – which proved how difficult it was to measure a moving target. Imagine watching raindrops fall: you pick one out and track its rapid descent through the air, but at the last minute it swerves violently away. That, according to Lucretius, is how the world works, predictable up to a point, but profoundly unpredictable beyond. It was – and it remains – a radical theory, and it helped reinforce the terms of that debate between the world as fundamentally orderly and fundamentally chaotic, a place you can or can't prepare for.

But what is radical about Lucretius's theory is more than the unsettling sense of chance it evokes, or the difficulty it implies in nailing down the laws of physics. There is an existential aspect too, for if chaos prevails it would seem to suggest one of two things: either there is no God – because God is the one who, in the first place, is supposed to have subdued chaos for the sake of order; or there is a God but he has absconded, defaulting on his duty and abandoning us mortals to take our chances in an unruly universe. In fact, the onus shifts on to us human beings in either case: in the absence of a divine father's stewardship, disorder seeps back into the world, and you have to ready, steady, gird yourself all the more.

But there is a twist. If, in the second scenario, God has failed to dot every i and cross every t, leaving us to get on with it, it might not necessarily be down to negligence. On the contrary, it might be a calculated form of care on his part, a 'tough love' of the theological variety. Imagine if he *had* put everything in order right down to the last iota, setting out a programme from the beginning of time to run in perpetuity. That would make us mere robots, reduced to dumbly acting out his project, and barely meriting the 'human' moniker we've been given. In simple terms, it would make getting ready in the morning as pointless as not: whatever you decide to do, God will have already mapped out your day, and any notion you had of being in control of it would be no more than illusion. In no meaningful sense would you be 'getting ready', because everything would be pre-prepared.

In other words, a little bit of possible 'negligence' by God goes a long way in creating human meaning, and it forms the basis for free will. To be properly human and worthy of the special status God has granted us, we have to have some headroom. We may be God's children, but we've got to be licensed as adults, with genuine choices and decisions to make. And for that to work, there have to be some things which cannot be anticipated and for which we can never be quite ready: if we were always absolutely ready every time we stepped out of the door, ready to the point of knowing exactly what the day had in store, there'd be none of those unforeseen choices – no spontaneous action to take, no judgement to exercise, no responsibility to assume and no call on our humanness. The fact that you could always be a bit more prepared – the fact, therefore, that you can never be 100 per cent ready in the morning – is very good, because it means that up its sleeve the day hides surprises, and each time it pulls one out, you have to think on your feet: you'll be required to use some in-the-moment discretion, which will reveal a human, an adult and a noble freedom on your part.

It's in another philosophical poem, Milton's *Paradise Lost*, where the argument for the freedom of the will – or the desirability of unreadiness – is made most eloquently, and located in the figure of Eve. Where Shakespeare's Cleopatra symbolises womanly experience, Milton's Eve is all innocence, tragically unprepared as she is for her seduction by the Devil. You could say she is the very icon of not-being-ready. Unguarded beside the apple tree in the Garden of Eden, and unaccompanied by Adam, Eve allows herself to be tempted by a walking, talking snake who is that selfsame Devil in disguise. She eats the fruit that God has forbidden, talks Adam into following suit, and in so doing triggers the Fall of Man. As Milton succinctly says, 'all creation wept'. So where is the upside?

Although her disobedience is tragic, Eve's innocence is not all bad. Certainly, that innocence leads her to make a poor choice – the very worst – but the fact that she makes a choice at all, the fact that she engages the Devil in a debate which could go either way, the fact that she acts without God breathing down her neck – all speak to her free will or, what amounts to the same thing, her margin for error. It is from this margin for error that freedom springs, because you can't be free to be right unless you can be free to be wrong. And since you can't be free to be wrong if you're always prepared, you shouldn't worry about getting completely ready in the morning. Yes, the more you prepare, the more you reduce your own likelihood of error, which is good; but the more you reduce your likelihood of error, the more you roll back your freedom, which is bad. The trick is to set the tension between the two forces at an optimum, like getting a good balance of bass and treble.

It's hard to conceive of getting ready to go out without also suppos-ing a putting on of clothes, and after waking up to the new, but fallen, horizon, Eve's first instinct is to cover her shame, thus establishing the cardinal function of getting dressed. Fig leaves are deployed about the loins, and while the symbolic weight of this first covering up is immense – the implication is that the naked world of truth and innocence is being left behind for the compromised world of disguise or deceit – it doesn't outweigh the more fundamental purpose to dressing, which is to mask the genitalia and seal off the organs of temptation that got Adam and Eve into trouble. In preparing to leave heaven and enter earth, in getting ready for the big wide world, they find it necessary, above all, to divert attention from the parts which were now a reminder of their fall from grace, an objective best served by fitting themselves out with some clothing.

And the objective has endured. Of course, not every single society today still upholds the beliefs that gave rise to clothing, or counts the public display of the private parts as taboo; but in the vast majority, apart from providing basic warmth and protection, the primary driver behind getting dressed remains the same as it was for our heavenly parents. Clothes exist to hide the pubic from the public and thereby make you socially acceptable. The irony is that, precisely because they are a prerequisite for social inclusion, wearing clothes has become almost more natural than being naked – an irony that caused Thomas Carlyle, the Victorian historian, to complain that the whole history of thought had 'tacitly figured man as a *Clothed Animal*; whereas he is by nature a *Naked Animal*'. Clothes are nothing less than our second skin.

To that established irony, we can add a more subtle one. As anyone who has been on a date well knows, clothes aren't just about covering you up: while you need them to hide your sex, you want them to show your sexuality. Even if you're just getting dressed for work in the morning, your clothes serve contradictory purposes. On the one hand, they do the job of masking your body; but on the other hand, they 'say' something about you, and you want them to speak well: you want them to make you attractive. Again it's a matter of keeping two forces in mutual tension – one that suppresses and another that expresses your sexual qualities. And depending on whether you're dressing for work or a date, you'll adjust the dials accordingly.

So, as long as your sexuality is literally dressed up as something else, it can be safely advertised in public – you just need to adapt to your particular audience. In this sense, clothes constitute the actual fabric in which the warp of society and the weft of sexuality are woven together. As such, they offer a perfect example of what Sigmund Freud called 'sublimation' – the indirect expression of libido, or the channelling of sexual energy into civilised form. In the language of psychoanalysis, sublimation reconciles the needs of the 'ego', or what I want for myself, with those of the 'superego', which is our sense of what the outside world requires of us. Banal as it seems, getting ready is that point in the day when the rivalry between the two needs is likely to peak, because we are making the transition from being at home and pleasing ourselves (ego) to going out and having to conform to a series of norms and conventions (superego). We become less ego and more superego with each button we fasten.

If we always button downwards rather than upwards, or pull on our underpants before our socks, and generally do things in our own way, it's because, according to Freud, the ego adores routine. Sure, the ego wants to please itself, but perversely it does so not by seeking out pleasure – which can cause it overexcitement – but by reducing 'unpleasure', which Freud defines as anything that throws the ego off course, upsetting its equilibrium. Even when it comes to something as ostensibly pleasurable as sex, what the ego likes about it is not the climax itself, but the removal of desire it affords – because desire as such is perturbing and importunate. As if it had a 'Do Not Disturb' sign hanging around its neck, the ego wants a quiet life, preferring flatness to spikes, lakes to mountains, schedules to surprises, and that translates into our tendency to form habits, to develop routines like the ones we go through every morning as we get ready. Holding change in abeyance, it prefers things the way they were.

All of which sounds eminently dull, does it not, except that the safe methods of sameness harbour within them a tendency to madness.

For while this liking for routine is the sign of a healthy ego blocking out disruption in order to preserve its steady state, it's a preference that perches at the top of a slippery slope which ends, alarmingly, in obsession – to put it bluntly, OCD (obssessive compulsive disorder) is just exaggerated routine. Because your morning ritual – shit, shower and shave, let's say – is largely undeviating, something you rehearse more or less automatically every day, you are never more than so many steps away from unhealthy repetitiousness. What if you start adding ritualistic components to your shower schedule, like lining up the shampoo bottles in a certain order? Does it mean you've gone the tiniest bit mad? Where does the normal shade into the abnormal? One of the characteristics we look for in 'normal' behaviour is that it is not too volatile, that it exhibits a high degree of dependability, but in its potential to lead you astray the most dependable behaviour in the world is also the most dangerous. Maybe that's not so bad: as you stand there in the bathroom again tomorrow morning, flossing or combing or applying deodorant, and lamenting how samey your life has become, you can take comfort in the fact that, far from being stuck in a rut, your psyche is much more interesting than it seems.

And even if there truly is something suspect in the fastidiousness you bring to the morning ritual, that ritual is also a rite, a spiritual exercise by which the whole of your body, and not just your eyes, becomes a window to your soul. Wherever getting clean is involved, a sacred element never lags far behind – they say, for example, that among advanced yogis the practice exists of excreting the bowel and macerating it in milk to cleanse it. Cleanliness, after all, is supposedly next to godliness, one of the few physical proxies available to us for spiritual worth. Which isn't to say that washing the body is any substitute for purifying the soul – you could even be accused of concentrating on outer virtues at the expense of inner ones – but it works as an important prerequisite. Long before Milton, for example, one of the oldest known, if anonymous, poems in English literature called itself 'Cleanness', and it took the connection between physical and spiritual purity to the limit: 'cleanness' was a reference to being clean of sin, whereas sin is figured as a spot or a stain. All of which suggests that being clean is more than simply desirable for stepping out into the world; it's essential for entering into heaven, and so it applies to death as much as life – hence the preparations of the corpse which involve its purification by water. By virtue of that act upon the dead body, the soul is ab-solved, just as if the sins were dis-solved, in a solution.

All well and good, you may say, but why this bias towards cleanliness as part of getting ready, as intrinsic to being prepared? When Mark Antony goes on *his* first date with Cleopatra, for example, he's reported not just to have scrubbed up, but to have shaved three times. Readiness and cleanliness appear as tied together as Antony and Cleopatra themselves. But why? Why can't you be ready and unclean? Why can't you be dirty, especially if a bit of dirt provides evidence of your having undergone something, and therefore being all the more geared up for whatever the day will throw at you? Why put on clean kit to play football, or a fresh apron to bake a cake? Not only will they get dirty again pretty quickly, but, even if you go out in clean clothes, have you really done anything to see off the dirt that's around you? Isn't dirt like energy, something you can displace but never destroy? There's no elimination of dirt per se, there's only a relocation of it, and the grease that washes off you down into the drain of the shower in the morning is on an endless journey that will see it dissolve and reappear in another combination of atoms elsewhere.

Disheartening as that sounds, there's something about the need for getting clean as part of getting ready which continues to withstand all rational objections, and very few of us leave home in the morning without some act, however mechanical, of self-purification. I suspect it's to do with aspiration – a word that, like respiration and inspiration, shares the same linguistic root as 'spirit', and all are to do with breathing in more life. The point of getting clean in the morning is to create a blank canvas on which something better than yesterday can be painted, and more life can be lived. In which case, who better to endorse the point than French writer Francis Ponge, whose very name translates as 'sponge', and who says in a eulogy to cleanness, called *Soap*: 'The exercise of soap will have left you cleaner, purer and sweeter-smelling than you were before ... it has changed you for the better, re-qualified you.' Ponge makes it clear that being clean helps you to create a brand-new start and aim again at your aspirations. For those aspirations to be abetted, for life to fare well, and for the day to succeed, we have to wash away what's gone before, as if an act of destruction had always to precede an act of creation.

And if in this rite of purification that surrounds getting ready there is a link from the body to the soul, there is a link from the body to the mind as well. Being ready involves wiping the mental slate clean, going forward without prejudice in order to be open to learning, and therefore applying the kind of razor to the overgrowth of our assumptions that became so famously associated with the medieval philosopher William of Ockham. 'Ockham's razor' is a kind of motto in philosophy that cautions against adding too much detail before you've seen the big picture; it says that the simplest explanation is usually the best. It implies shaving away your preconceptions so that you are ready to see things more barely and more clearly. It even refers back to the idea of free will: rather than having wisely prepared all future events to his own recipe, God has shaved most of the concealing façade of prediction away in order to allow humans to grow the future for themselves. The day takes on more meaning the less it is decided in advance; and shaving in the morning creates virgin territory on which the day might cultivate itself in all sorts of unpredictable ways.

In this, our ritual of getting clean in the morning also implies we are 'meliorists' – optimists, essentially, who bear a deep assumption not only that the world can be better, but that we can make it better by making ourselves better. And it is just such meliorism that numbers among the many emotions Cleopatra feels when she talks about an 'armour of gold' for Antony. In her heart of hearts, she probably knows that he is doomed (and she too), but the prospect of glory is hard to resist. How much better, in any case, it is to bow out with a flourish than die in a ditch. So if getting ready in the morning has a defensive subtext, it's about putting on the ritz regardless – gladrags are for wearing in the rain. Yes, when we're getting ready, we're going to do battle in an uncertain world, which requires a certain seriousness because the risks are not always trivial, but what's the harm in going out in style? It's not just that offence is the best form of defence, but that fighting the unknown with a sense of glamour carries its own redemption. God may not be there to rescue you, but if it all goes horribly wrong, at least you'll have gone out prepared in your silks and finery, victim to the very thing – the sense of chance – that made the life you've just relinquished worth living.

3

Travelling to work

T. S. ELIOT COMPARED entering the London underground with going down into the circles of hell, and wrote of descending 'only/Into the world of perpetual solitude'. Like subways around the world, it is a world of spiritual deprivation where there are lots of people but no contact of any worth, endless 'twitter' that fails to generate meaning, and a great deal of hurry serving only to defer the stillness your soul requires to flourish.

OK, your journey to work might not be quite so desolate – some commutes involve a stroll over the bridge or a cycle through the park. And for that expanding class of people who work from home, there's no commute at all, beyond a soft-shoe shuffle after breakfast from kitchen towards desk. In fact, these 'telecommuters' sometimes lament having no journey to work or office to aim at – not just because at home they develop cabin fever, but because the journey has the power to legitimise the work they do and make it seem more 'proper'. The time spent travelling also creates a boundary between home and work that the homeworker – obliged to answer the door to the gasman, or ask the children to be quiet – sometimes craves.

But for many of those who do have to travel to work, the morning commute spells drudgery. What's worse, it forms part of a larger misery that Parisians have nicknamed 'métro, boulot, dodo' – the eternal and apparently meaningless cycle of commuting, working and sleeping into which we almost unconsciously fall. There's a reason why being a commuter evokes hamsters on a wheel or rats in a race: in focusing on our destination, we lose contact with our destiny. So is there any way of breaking out?

The answer is yes, but only so long as we wean ourselves off what Nietzsche – he's the man on the train sitting opposite with the bushy moustache and intense eyes – called the 'doctrine of two worlds'. This is the doctrine whereby we invent an ideal world to escape the one we're in. While living out our Groundhog Day existence, we imagine giving it all up and starting a vineyard in Tuscany; packed like sardines in the train carriage, we picture sailing around the Maldives. The fantasies might be consoling, but we invent them, says Nietzsche, only because we can't stand the fact that this is all there is; and having invented them, we do little to bring them about. Which means our fantasies are a sign of weakness, prompting Nietzsche to respond with a challenge that is simple, if not easy: make your ideal a reality or – slightly preferable – your reality ideal. To that end he'd ask you to imagine repeating your life in every single detail – including this oppressive train ride – and how much of it you could bear. Only when you get to the point where each moment is one you'd happily relive would he let you off the hook – the point at which your two worlds merge. Assuming that this newly integrated, single world is one in which you haven't given up your job, your journey to work becomes a joy.

Getting to such a point means you both leave behind what Nietzsche calls 'the herd' – those in cattle class, effectively – and join the league of 'supermen', that elite who have kept not just their destination but their destiny in mind and made themselves the masters of it. Belonging to this club brings two benefits. First, ditching the fantasy of another world means you're more likely to invest in this one: you will live for the moment, rather than speculating on a heaven to save you from yourself; and there's nothing like having the crutch of the ideal snatched away for making you plunge into reality in all its bracing nudity. Not only will you see things for what they are, unadorned but all the more intense for it, you'll no longer be cowed by some ideal to which you feel you ought to conform – wherein lies benefit number two. Precisely because it's *ideal*, the ideal holds the high office of prescribing how things should be; it follows that once you are relieved of the canopy it throws above your head, you'll be free to become yourself in all your nonconformist individuality – jagged, singular, wayward, defiant, eccentric, bold, unorthodox and original. For that, giving up on the ideal might be a price worth paying.

Luckily, there are also less demanding ways of taking up Nietzsche's gauntlet. All it really requires is getting to work in one piece. Simply by being the same person at the end of your journey to work as you were when you left home, you become identifiable as you, and therefore attain a distinctive identity – which renders surplus to requirements the heroic act of self-confirmation that Nietzsche extols. Even as you fall in with the stolid rhythm of a hundred other feet stomping down the street towards the office, ever on the point of blending in with the crowd, you'll find it very hard not to keep on being you; with every step, your identity will be restated, your sameness stamped on every stone. Far from having to execute some cunning stunt of self-actualisation, you can, just by leaving home each morning and arriving at the other end, pretty much stumble into an identity that is yours and yours alone. Maybe that identity won't qualify for the rank of Nietzschean superman – and your life won't be any less ordinary – but nothing's going to stop it continuously confirming itself. In this sense, your making it to work as you and not someone else counts as a minor triumph.

It's a triumph that doesn't happen entirely unaided, however. It depends on the services of an invisible angel whose name is time. For you to acquire identity, you have to remain the same *as yourself*: the person who arrives at your workstation to unlock your computer has to be the same person who locked your door on the way out. Which sounds obvious, but throws up the philosophical and scientific problem of comparing something with itself – it's not like comparing an apple with an orange, for example, which you can put side by side.

Thankfully, though, you're not restricted to comparing yourself in space, like the apple and the orange – you can compare yourself with yourself over time instead. Imagine, for example, leaving for work with your partner: he will take the train and you will cycle, and you agree to meet for a quick coffee at the other end. When he gets there, his curly hair hasn't suddenly straightened and his eyes are the shade of green they always were: he's definitely the guy you live with. The angel of time has inserted a gap before your seeing him again, allowing his identity to be confirmed. Identity is about being recognised – *re*cognised, that is, after such a break.

But the angel is also a demon. What if, when your partner walks into Starbucks an hour after you left home together, his hair has grown six inches and his eyes have turned brown? Is he the same man? It's a theme explored most vividly in the film *The Return of Martin Guerre*, which retells the true story of a sixteenth-century French peasant who goes off to work in the fields one morning and doesn't come back. Time passes and six years later he – or someone claiming to be him – returns, to take up again with his wife. The villagers duly compare the returning Martin with their mental image of the departing Martin (the camera hasn't yet been invented), and the match is never quite perfect. He looks a lot like the man who left, but whether it's the real Martin or an impostor, no one can definitively say, and the question divides the village (in a further twist, the peasant's actual surname was not Guerre but Daguerre, as in daguerreotype, which, as the first form of photograph, is a copy of an original). As such, the film portrays the wicked side of time, whose role as medium of identity coincides with its role as medium of difference. Just as you need time to be able to remain the same and be identified as yourself, you also need time to be able to change, which is where your identity suddenly gets less stable. That is why, even as your hair turns grey, you have the same glint in your eye that your mum would recognise from when you were a child.

All of this means that if you do arrive at work as the same person who left your house, it's somewhat a matter of chance. Or, put the other way round, if, on the matter of identity, time is as likely to subvert as substantiate it, then even the journey to work, mundane as it is, must leave you open to the risk of change. Just because it's mundane, that doesn't mean your identity isn't in play, for anything could happen en route to cause that identity to be refashioned: you could lose a limb in a car crash, read an article that shifts your political opinions, or receive a call to say that your job's being relocated to another country. Think too of the TV images of people getting off a plane who've been involved in an engine blow-out or near-miss or a hijack – looking at their haunted expressions, you can see the experience has altered them. Equally, the transfigurations can be wondrous: on that seemingly everyday journey, you might one day fall in love and step off on to the platform with your face shining.

What this teaches us in turn is that things going right and things going wrong are not opposites, and the journey to work proves the point; if things have worked out as you planned, you were lucky. Captured in a coinage by the French philosopher Jacques Derrida – who had a soft spot for cars – it is the law of 'destinerrance', which says that unless it's possible for you to be diverted, it's impossible for you to arrive at your destination; for you to make the journey at all means being at the mercy of both outcomes, both arriving and failing to arrive, and you can't get off first base unless all bets are on. Going on a journey means just that – the spirit of adventure, which harbours the possibility of being blown off course, floats above us all, no matter what maps we use. St Christopher, patron saint of travellers, finds himself eternally shadowed by this more mercurial genie.

So much for ourselves. But we rarely travel to work in isolation, and of all our daily experiences, travelling to work is the one most likely to bring us into contact with others. Particularly if your work takes place in a city, the journey there makes it painfully evident that you share the world with a multitude of people – often thousands of them – and most of us have probably experienced the humbling sensation of being just one in a crowd. We know what Nietzsche's response would be – assert yourself all the more aggressively – and we know that even if you shy away from Nietzschean self-fashioning, you can distinguish yourself from others almost without trying, just by showing up at work as usual – albeit that your identity will have been quietly under threat along the way. But how else might we think about this daily contact – sometimes quite physical contact – with strangers?

Of course, as a phenomenon, the crowd has upsides as well as downsides – if at its worst a crowd reverts to its lowest common denominator, or the brute mentality that results in people being stampeded to death, then at its best a crowd becomes the organised resource that can raise a barn and be more than the sum of its parts. It's not exactly a crowd, however, but something more complex that we are navigating among when we go to work in the morning. That's because on a motorway surging with southbound cars or on a train of stressed-out commuters, an unspoken competitiveness prevails, and the sense of common purpose never quite comes together. Yes, everyone's on their way to work, and all are aimed at the same task of earning a crust, but because work is about competing and therefore differentiating yourself once more from others, the crowd that goes to work is tacitly engaged in a war of all against all that sometimes continues even after you've made it into the office. You're all on your way to work, but work is about getting ahead, or putting clear water between you and those others you both respect and, frankly, despise. And while you will need to cooperate with your fellow travellers in order for society to function – you can't all go through the ticket barrier at once – you pretty much always want to be first.

When people talk about fighting their way to work, in other words, it's more than metaphor – there's a real, if veiled, sense of winners and losers, of victors and victims, that runs beneath it; and 'the war of all against all' carries implications more ponderous than simply making the so-called rush hour slow. As a phrase it hails from Thomas Hobbes, writing in the seventeenth century at a time of bur-geoning democracy, a time when the grip of the monarchy and landed gentry was weakening and the frame of the world was creaking with a free market (the invention of credit, the liquidation of noble estates, the imperial expansion of trading routes) butting like a bull at its sides – the free market being the very thing that so many people are commuting towards when they head to work in the morning. It's a prospect that brought Hobbes out in a philosophical rash: left to its own devices, the crowd – the pack of individuals competing with one another – that teems to work over the Hudson or the Seine, the Tiber or the Thames, in pursuit of personal gain, would turn on itself and civil war break out. To head off such a prospect, we must put in place some means of keeping the peace.

In effect, Hobbes is describing exactly the cusp between order and chaos that obtains during the morning commute. On the one hand, there's a swell of latent aggression, the urge to elbow your way ahead of others, with everyone in it for themselves. On the other hand, we consent to and obey those mechanisms of control which are placed around us, and chief among these is the red light. Whether we're crossing the road as a pedestrian, cruising down it on a bicycle or stuck on a train held up by a signal, the red light on the way to work serves a function that's more than logistical. It says that everyone's entitled to their turn, and if you run into red after red you know that, over the course of your life, it will even out, and you'll get as many lights that are green. So the red light's regulation of the journey to work is in large measure to do with fairness, and you're reminded of this lofty principle every workday morning as you wait for the lights to change.

But the red light is also to do with authority and in this it's a purely Hobbesian device. Because the red light ultimately lets you have a fair turn it would be foolish to think it repressive – and yet its authority is hard to deny. Yes, you can jump a red light, but you don't win by doing so – your conscience pricks you, for you know the red light's authority is incontestable. Why is that? Because its authority is depersonalised or abstract, and far more powerful, say, than that of a traffic cop whose humanness makes his authority that little bit more debatable – he's only one of us, after all. And abstract authority is precisely what Hobbes said all societies need to protect themselves from themselves, from having out their disagreements at that purely human or inter-personal level where it's just my word against yours. By entrusting ourselves to this abstract system of fairness which is embodied in the red light on the way to work, we save ourselves a lot of argument; in fact, we save ourselves from each other.

In the next chapter, I'll talk about being at work, but before finishing it's worth flagging an irony – that we sometimes put more effort into getting to work than into doing it. Now, that's partly because we have to: for all the frustrations at work, they tend to be far less visceral than those involved in your commute, and you're as likely to tell your partner about your horrible journey as about your difficult meeting. But it might also be because the art of work lies as much in showing up as in doing anything productive once you've arrived. One reason for trying so hard to get to work is to be able to say to your boss and your colleagues, 'Here I am! I made the effort to get here!' You've shown willing, and that goes a long way – no doubt too long – in proving that you're doing your job.

So there you are: you've passed through the shadowy world of the subway, all too conscious that it is, and you are, less than ideal; you're mostly certain that you're the same person you were who shut your front door an hour earlier; and you've narrowly avoided strangling your fellow passengers. Despite the odds, you've made it, and the office, the lab, the factory, the hospital, the school, the stadium looms into view. The next question is what it's all for.

4

Being at work

HAVE YOU EVER FANTASISED about quitting your job? About striding into your boss's office and telling him (it's more likely to be a man) what you think of him and his stinking business? About strolling back, after the deed, through the rows of desks, head held high, smugly accepting the looks of awed admiration on the faces of your colleagues? About walking out of the blasted building for the last time and into the sunshine of your new life?

If it's a fantasy you recognise, it reveals a number of things about you. First, and most obviously, you're in the wrong job. Second, if you haven't yet converted the fantasy into reality, you're a coward. Or, third, to be less harsh, you lack a safety net: you can't resign because you've got financial commitments – mortgage, rent, kids, debts, bills – and not enough spare cash to meet them. Finally, it says you belong with 66 per cent of the population.

According to a recent newspaper survey, 34 per cent of lottery millionaires prefer to keep their job. Assuming that, before the day of the jackpot, such people are pretty average, we can deduce that about a third of all those in work aren't there just for the money. Even if you adjust for the fact that per capita spending on the lottery is higher among lower social bands and that some players are already retired, this still leaves, say, a quarter of the working population who, following a windfall, would continue in the same employment. Far from biding their time at work until the big payout, when they can jack it all in, these people can't even be paid to go away. They keep working despite the fact that they don't need to. And that raises the question of what, exactly, work is all about.

In its most classic definition – the one that Marx was so radically to revise, as we'll see – work is the exchange of labour for money. And where money is involved, some force is at hand, some agency countering the drift of nature. For having to be paid implies you'd have preferred to stay in bed or go fishing, and so, for tolerating this unwelcome interruption to your leisure, you expect to be 'compensated'. A word not lacking in peculiar overtones – being 'compensated' for injury, say – 'compensation' nevertheless goes to the concept at the heart of work, which is that of *balance*: whenever that exchange of labour for money takes place, they ought to be equivalent. In this view, the purchase of labour is no different from buying sugar or envelopes, where the swapping of commodities for currency must be fair and the balance struck.

But for a quarter of the working population, those who in theory would work regardless of compensation, that balance could be said to be off, and it's a significant enough proportion to warrant some comment, both cruel and kind. The kinder interpretation says that those people who make up this demographic have nobly elevated work above pecuniary concerns. In work they see the opportunity for job satisfaction or personal fulfilment; and lest that sound selfish, in the best cases they perceive the work they do as 'giving something back' to society, doing their 'bit' or 'making a difference'. Although they continue to draw a salary, their labour counts almost as it would for a charity – a kind of free good, donated out of a sense of moral duty. As such, these people only bear out what other surveys consistently report: that employees look for not just financial reward but intangible benefits, such as the chance to be stretched or a sense of purpose.

And if all that sounds a bit goody-two-shoes, there is the crueller perspective. These are the people, after all, who whistle at their desks while the rest of you have your heads down, whose faces pop up over your cubicle with a shiny corporate smile. But let's set aside the *feelings* that this category of person must from time to time elicit from the majority who simply trade their labour for the money it equates to, and who don't enjoy the same serene relationship to working life as the magic quarter: there's a more rational basis for disliking them. Because this annoying minority permit themselves to be 'compensated' for something they would have done anyway, their vocation becomes a vacation, and they are getting a double yield on the effort invested – taking out twice what they put in once, and distorting the market. By hiking up the emotional value of the labour done in their organisation, they lower its monetary worth, such that their presence in the workplace will have a counter-inflationary impact, albeit subtle, on wages, and thus spoil it for the rest.

But whether you feel kindly or cruelly disposed towards them, this group deserves no more attention, obviously, than those at the other end of the bell curve, for whom the balance is off because they get paid *less* than what is fair. Though senior executives may claim that 'our people are our greatest assets', being at work can for many feel that the give-and-take is out of kilter, and in 'compensation' for all the hours plucking chickens, entering data or loading bags on to aircraft, there's little sense of being valued by the powers that be. Ironically, the word 'asset' gives it away: as in that other peculiar phrase from the modern workplace, 'human resources', it's clear that those who do the legwork are considered primarily as units of economic value, not as people.

Enter Karl Marx. Another name for the undercompensation for labour contributed is, not to beat about the bush, slave wages – meaning crudely what's paid to those people who put in a great deal more than what they get out. Marx had two key insights about this state of affairs. Most critically, he said it wasn't the result of economic accident, innate ability or natural process, but of specific social forces. If sections of the workforce are woefully underpaid for their labour, and this keeps them poor, it's not because that's just how it is, or because they're stupid, jinxed, racially inferior or lazy; it's to do with a chain of causes that can be traced back to their masters, who prosper at their expense. And – surprise, surprise – their masters are none other than those who get paid more than their labour is worth. Indeed, the fact that they get paid over the odds is what allows them to acquire their masterful power in the first place. The extra that they pocket – the handsome salary, the princely bonus – translates as capital, and with capital comes a panoply of mutually reinforcing benefits that others may well resent. Not that you have to be at the bottom of the pile to feel the injustice in what Marx is describing – plenty of middle managers will look wanly across to the boss's corner office and wonder if the work being done in it truly justifies being paid so much more.

Although discussions of capital can be intricate and contentious, it's this being paid more than what's fair that lies at the bottom of things. Even if it's tied up in shares or land, capital is spare money, and this is precisely why for the poor, who have nothing to spare, capital remains an elusive prize: only once you've satisfied your immediate needs can you turn to building up your asset base. But should you be fortunate enough to scale this golden first rung of the ladder, the pre-eminent benefit that capital brings is the chance to secure your own position, not least by investing that same capital in order to multiply it, and in so doing putting more height between you and those you've left behind. You can even look forward to the compound interest that Baron Rothschild declared the eighth wonder of the world. For this is the other key aspect of capital – it's about growth, about making more of itself from itself, like yeast, the magic ingredient that the capitalist hungrily pursues. As for the workers, well, let them eat bread.

At that point, it only gets worse, for this vertical stretch that capital creates between rich and poor then gets played out in society as class difference – as if there were indeed some natural order of things, rather than the brute fact of capital driving society apart into separate classes. What we call 'class', in other words, is an excuse for the economic disparities that prevail, an excuse that makes those disparities falsely appear as inevitable. But if all that sounds rather desperate, it brings Marx to his second key insight, which holds the possibility of redemption or revenge – that the rich can't do without the poor, so the poor have hidden strength.

Inspired by Hegel's investigations into the relationship between masters and slaves, which found that masters are masters only to the extent that they are recognised as such by those they dominate, Marx isolated a more basic truth: one man's wealth is another man's poverty, meaning that the rich depend on the poor, and the poor, in a reversal of roles, take on a certain power. Rather than letting this power be squandered, Marx encouraged the poor to exploit it, and to do so by presenting their labour not as cheap but as indispensable – it is the workers, after all, who 'own the means of production'. And while the most direct method of highlighting the value of your labour is to withhold it by striking – we all know how valuable a dustman becomes when he's not collecting our rubbish – there are profounder energies in train. The other lesson Marx learned from Hegel was that history, like a comet, was on an unalterable course, with its destination as truth, where truth is a state in which masters and slaves see themselves in each other's eyes, and realise no difference – none are more equal than others. Society having climbed up to this plateau, the ladder of inequality would be thrown away and a commune would prevail. Going on strike might give a spur to the process, and a coup d'état might act as catalyst, but in either case the communist state is a foregone conclusion to which the sophomore practices of capital must irresistibly yield. Slaves – the bulk of the workforce – have nothing to lose but their chains.

In the face of so trenchant a formulation, how could one possibly see capital as anything but evil, or work as anything other than the feral sizing up between haves and have-nots? Are you not justified in loathing your overpaid, overfed directors? Shouldn't you be joining a union and marching for fairer pay?

The answer is that not only might capital not be evil, it might be the very flower of virtue. At least, this is the answer put forward by Max Weber, who himself grew up in an affluent family and helped launch the discipline of sociology. If capital is the money left over from your wage packet after you've paid your bills, it's just the consequence, according to Weber, of hard work. Far from being indicted for your wealth, you may deserve to be venerated for it as testimony to your work ethic, and those directors got to where they are not by luck but by graft. As Jack Welch, former boss of General Electric, once said, 'The harder I work, the luckier I get.' What's more, if you don't then blow it on Friday night, this hard-earned wedge speaks to your abstemiousness – an abstemiousness which led Weber, whose mother was a strict Calvinist, to point out its affinity with Protestantism, which stresses the conjoint virtues of labour and self-denial. That these virtues combine so effectively to produce cash is a rich irony, of course, especially as cash per se continues to be considered filthy. Cash is flash, which is one of the reasons it needs to be buried, hidden, deposited in a vault where its value can grow in the dark. The protest which gave Protestantism its name was against display, against the staginess of the Catholic Church, and its aversion to theatrics applies equally to money: better to appear less wealthy than you are and keep putting in the hours. It's the quiet types in the office who will have the last laugh.

Suddenly, the definition of work as the plain exchange of labour for money seems simplistic. Either that exchange is unfair, which creates a two-tier system run by self-interested masters (Marx), or it is fair, but still dominated by masters – those who have learned self-denial (Weber). In this respect, both thinkers were suspicious of what 'mastery' consisted in, and Weber went on to consider what mastery in the workplace – or 'leadership' – might mean.

He broke it down into three categories, of which 'charismatic' leadership has become best known. Today, we tend to think of charisma as a positive, a special quality that certain people enviably possess – you may have worked for a boss, say, who had a natural charm and persuasiveness that you just couldn't help going along with; you might even have wanted to earn their pride and gone the extra mile. But for Weber and those he influenced, charisma has a dark side. Like a secret ingredient, it is as elusive as it is desirable, not a skill that can be learned; and when the top jobs are appointed, it's often the indefinable qualities, rather than anything on the CV, that make the difference. Which is dangerous, because it implies that people with oodles of charisma can get away with a gap in basic competence, even using that charisma as a veil from behind which they manipulate others. Worse still, it's a manipulation we collude with: the 'charisma' of the leader, says Weber, is as much to do with the superstitious yearnings of those whom the leader leads as with any innate merits. Standing by the water cooler, we gossip about the boss because he's the boss, and the gossip only reinforces the sense of his being special; even if secretly we know he's dull as dishwater, we can't help attributing a mysteriousness to him, which says more about our own need for someone on whom to fixate.

Thankfully, leadership comes in less ominous varieties, and it is Weber's 'rational-legal' type that applies more broadly to modern-day work. True, some businesses still revolve around Weber's third type of leadership – the 'traditional', which takes the form of a patriarch in charge of his family, or the feudal lord overseeing his demesne – but the nature and scale of modern commerce are such that the most efficient way of its being organised is as a bureaucracy, which is where 'rational-legal' leadership comes in, and where the leader gets redefined not as a charismatic presence but as a competent official whose authority is underpinned by rules rather than by personality. Today it's rare, of course, to hear the word 'bureaucracy' spoken without disdain, but if only because it attenuates the abuse of power implicit in the other two types it's not so dreadful. You might experience it as stifling, but, like democracy, bureaucracy might offer the 'least bad' solution to the problem of processing the concerns of a large number of people.

Bureaucracy in turn has several features, and the one you'll recognise instantly from being at work is hierarchy. If organisations have hierarchies (and which organisation doesn't have at least an unofficial one?), it is more for 'rational-legal' than charismatic reasons – that is, it's not to pin certain workers higher up the league table than others (although that is the by-product), it's because volumes of work are best handled by a pyramid structure. The most transactional tasks can be done by the least skilled workers, but their relative lack of skill means they need directing by the next layer above and so on. And in case you're thinking, like Marx, this is a covert means of reasserting class difference, a hierarchy, as in the command-and-control structure of the armed forces, simply facilitates the fastest transmission of instructions with the smallest amount of the 'friction' (as they call it in the army) that comes with consultation or debate. If it excludes the opinions of juniors, it's only to expedite the work itself, whose needs are straightforward, implacable and relentless. In other words, if you find yourself some way from the top when it comes to hierarchies, you shouldn't take it personally.

That likening of the commercial organisation to an army has dwindled, of course – 'human resources' was once known as 'personnel' – and today we reach for more organic terms – the 'living system', for example, or 'organisational DNA'. But the change in language has hardly managed to put an end to hierarchies at work, and a modern apologia for them is made by Elliott Jaques, the management guru (a phrase which for some will be an oxymoron). Before praising hierarchy, however, Jaques blames teams. Writing at the end of the twentieth century, he was in a position to reflect back coolly on post-war evolutions in the workplace that promoted the notion of teamworking – this being the very notion to which hierarchy finds itself least reconciled – as a panacea.

At first sight, the team seems like a good idea, and if you've ever worked in one you might have experienced a pleasing sense of belonging – so much so, perhaps, that you felt more loyalty to it than to the organisation of which it was a part. Because the team recognises and harnesses diverse talents, it reflects advances in wider society: the expansion of liberal democracy, the formalising of human rights, the extension to minorities of suffrage and the broadening of welfare – all good things, no doubt. It even parallels the rise of the focus group and the emergence of group therapy as vehicles for its members to express themselves. So saturated has 'team' become with these Western values of inclusion, in fact, that to laud the relative merits of 'hierarchy' is seen almost as a vote for fascism ... And while 'team' is the single word that captures most tightly the post-war abhorrence of authoritarian practice, its most obvious reference, of course, is to sport – when it comes to business-speak, sporting metaphors are surely the most ubiquitous of all ('pulling together', 'getting onside', etc.). No doubt sports lingo serves in part to glamorise what is essentially unglamorous office work, but its general verve contributes to an esprit de corps that is more conducive to getting work done. If a team at work can mobilise itself like a high-performing sports team, deep resources of discretionary energy may be released. Taken together, all those factors make the team a sacred cow in the workplace – try telling your boss you're not a 'team player' and see how long you last.

Despite all those general advantages, to Elliott Jaques the team fails to deliver on its promise. When they come together, the individuals in it add up to less than the sum of their parts, and that's mainly because the spreading of effort across several people leads both to a diffusion of accountability and to a confusion of role. In a team, you can hide. Everyone and no one is responsible, and when the meeting ends it's not clear who's supposed to be doing what. Even if mutual understanding has been gained, the work – the very thing the team was set up to process more ably – gets lost. What's worse, the 'team' remains assembled when there's no match being played, which means it's not even a team so much as a convenient grouping that ends up making work for itself.

It is in the face of this tendency that Jaques recommends the use of hierarchy. If the raison d'être of an organisation is to do work – rather than provide an environment for socialising – then work is best served by that line running through that organisation down which the boss can see the stopping of the buck is on its staged ascent to, or descent from, himself. At every level, the work is properly 'owned' and, where owned, more likely to be finished; teams are OK so long as the work within them is clearly apportioned, and the team has an identifiable leader (in this sense, the dichotomy between teams and hierarchy is false). Devoid of political, social or psychological features, hierarchy is but the form that such ownership needs to take; the boss removes his mask as bogeyman, becoming merely the prudent guarantor of the work's passage through the management layers. The 'organisation' stands more for the way the work, rather than the workforce, needs to be organised, and once the work is restored to this rightful place, everything can proceed.

Sadly, few organisations run so smoothly. It's not that they don't have the skeleton that a hierarchy provides, but that they are also made of flesh. Because they are composed of humans, history and habit, they can't be reduced to either the hierarchy or the work shuttling up and down it; and it is this excess in organisations of other factors, over and above those they might be stripped down to, that we know as office politics. The result is that being at work requires us to negoti-ate a weird combination of formal rule and informal reality, what is preached and what is practised, business acumen and blind emotion. I wrote earlier about 'compensation' and for this aspect of work alone the word – otherwise unnatural – is spot on: for putting up with all the nonsense that comes with office politics, some compensation seems precisely what is due. Which brings us back full circle, to what work is and the appropriate recompense for it.

In response to the creeping growth of the service economy, Marga-ret Thatcher famously said that not everybody can take in everybody's washing – somebody has to make the clothes. But the service – or 'knowledge' – economy can't have been listening, because in the gen-eration after, it only self-seeded. In professional services, the analogue of doing the laundry might be 'consultancy'; in the public sector, 'part-nership working'; and even the manufacturing industry hasn't been sheltered from the duty of 'client relationship management', whereby a car producer, for example, must 'engage' its 'stakeholders' about its plans and their impact on them. In all cases, it's hard to pin down exactly what the work is, or why anyone should therefore be paid for it. Its chief mode, after all, is talking, and for anyone who believes that employment should employ the hands – in ploughing, sowing, reaping, milking, making, fixing, cutting, stitching, shaping, lifting, shifting – the concept of being paid to talk must appear bizarre and even unjust. And that doesn't even take into account the fact that a significant amount of the actual activity in offices isn't even talking but doing emails (not just writing them, but deleting them, re-sending them, recalling them, and so on). Add on the reality that workers will also chat to one another, call home, make tea and visit the WC and you begin to wonder how much *work* work they do. A further survey, conducted by a management magazine, found that US workers spend thirty minutes a day just looking for things in order to be able to do their job. It's clear that 'working' and 'being at work' overlap, but only up to a point.

And yet perhaps that spaceship-like gliding further into the intangible is not as irreversible as we've come to believe. Perhaps we are on the verge of what Michel Foucault, the French social historian, called an 'epistemic break'. Not dissimilar to a 'paradigm shift', an epistemic break marks a watershed in history where a new frame for looking at the world interposes itself: Karl Marx's reframing of history as the history of class struggle, for example, was one such break. Perhaps the current crisis in resources of the staple kind – fuel, water, food – will lead to a correction of this drift towards ever more abstract forms of working. As the cost of such basics rises, so our spending on services declines and we focus once more on what's real. That could have a knock-on effect on being at work, where we'll be asked to demonstrate not 'added value' so much as the basic worth of what we're producing. Who knows, but perhaps work will swing back to a more fundamental form, one that involves less talking and more honest labour-like collecting hay into bundles, driving rivets into the hull of a ship or darning socks.

5

Going to the doctor

AS WE KNOW, humour doesn't always travel: what makes the Russian roar with laughter leaves the Somali stony-faced, and vice versa. But some jokes manage to vault over national boundaries.

> A man calls the doctor: 'Doctor, what should I do? My friend just keeled over and died!'
> 'The first thing is to make sure he's definitely dead.'
> 'OK, hold on …' A gunshot sounds. 'Now what?'

It may not be as surreally funny as the joke depicted in *Monty Python* – which, because it made people die from laughing, was deployed by the army – but in a study of gags with universal appeal, this came top. The sense of helplessness in an emergency, the miscommunication between doctor and caller, its tragic consequence and the eager ingenuousness of the final question – the joke arranges them all to provoke in its audience an emotion that is simultaneously unbearable and exquisite. Among doctor jokes, this is a peach.

But why so many more jokes about doctors than vets, say, or gardeners? We tend to joke about things that make us nervous, and in the case of doctors, what makes us nervous is probably their authority. As the great critic Maurice Blanchot writes in an extraordinary story about being in hospital, 'I liked the doctors quite well … The annoying thing was that their authority loomed larger by the hour. One is not aware of it, but these men are kings.' From the moment we address her (or him), we're aware of the doctor's authority; just to enunciate the word 'Doctor' – a title and not a name – is to put us on unequal terms. Whatever the ailment, it is to the doctor we go, because the doctor possesses the expertise we lack, and for all the efforts to modernise healthcare – whereby 'patient' becomes 'customer' and supposedly gains the upper hand – the disparity prevails. The doctor promises at least an insight into our condition, at most a cure, and the expectation thus created can hardly fail to give her the authoritative edge. Add the fact that that very condition puts us in the weaker position and you can see why we're at her mercy. Small wonder that the profession suffers from a malady of its own, an overweening arrogance known as 'God syndrome'.

The divine authority of the doctor draws from two sources, in fact, not just her expertise. The flipside of the doctor's insight is the patient's blindness: without our own uncertainty as patients about our condition, that authority would be halved. You could object that since the unofficial practice of Googling your symptoms began, and the official one of being encouraged to self-diagnose, we know more than ever about the inner workings of our body, and we're likely to arrive in the waiting room with as much data as the doctor herself; indeed, so much so that we are developing into just the 'expert patient' that, in the interests of devolving responsibility, health services want us to become. But no matter the depth of our private investigations, it's to the doc we turn to make the final judgement, and we do so not just because the office of doctor alone can pronounce on our physical fate, but also because, beyond a certain vanishing point, we're as incapable of appraising our own condition as we are of looking between our shoulder blades. Even if the thing is as visible to the naked eye as a rash, a gash or a bunion, our personal assessment is never quite enough; we feel it must be ratified. Allowing the accomplished doctor to throw our own analysis so suavely into relief therefore does two things: it reinforces her authority, for sure, but in doing so it defines the limit of our own, and suggests that without a third party we cannot see ourselves clearly. Some, like the Austrian philosopher Ivan Illich, have gone further and spoken of 'iatrogenesis', the phenomenon by which we're convinced of the need to take unnecessary medicines and become sicker as a result. For by giving so much authority over to the doctor, you ask yourself to be medicated as much as possible, in a process that exploits the incomplete self-knowledge we began with.

And as you let the doctor insert the syringe in your ear or examine your vertebrae, you might reflect on how odd this is, the fact that we need an extra pair of eyes to be able to see ourselves. If you accept that the body is not just the vehicle of the self – legs to bear us, arms to reach what we need – but its very substance, such that along with the mind the body constitutes the self that each of us is, our not being able without help to see properly into the body means we can't see properly into our selves. There's a part that will always elude us, a shadow that will fall across the otherwise transparent relationship each self enjoys with itself. While an appointment with the doctor illuminates our condition, the fact that we needed to consult her in the first place confirms that, when it comes to what we know about ourselves, we live in a state of partial eclipse. This is not necessarily a bad thing – if we could see all of ourselves all of the time, we might become as trapped in our bodies as hypochondriacs; a bit of self-unawareness probably allows us to boldly go into the world.

But odder than this partial invisibility to ourselves is the invisibility of the illness itself. In a book that combines literature, psychology and medicine, called *The Body in Pain*, leading American academic Elaine Scarry goes some way towards scoping out such invisibility:

When one hears about another person's physical pain, the events happening within the interior of that person's body may seem to have the remote character of some deep subterranean fact, belonging to an invisible geography that, however portentous, has no reality because it has not yet manifested itself on the visible surface of the earth.

Even if we have high levels of empathy, the other person's pain can't help but seem as abstract as the suffering we watch on TV – the way we become desensitised over time to images of flood victims, for example – and it's an abstraction, an invisibility or incomprehensibility, that applies as much to ourselves when we are in pain or suffering with an illness. Say, for example, the doctor makes the assessment that confirms or counters your own, bolsters her authority and duly sends you away – if not quite an open book to yourself, at least more enlightened than when you arrived. Say that, in doing so, she'll have drawn from the battery of scientific apparatus available to the modern medic – lasers, scanners, DNA sampling, probes, micro-cameras, computer analysis, 3D imaging, databases, robots – and pinpointed the very bacterium that's invaded you, the individual cell that's been corrupted, the particular chromosome that's lacking. Say, finally, that she's gone on to state the name – astigmatism, bradycardia, toxoplasmosis, melanoma, hepatitis – that sums the illness up. All well and good. If not yet physically contained by treatment, that illness has, by diagnosis, been rationally boxed off; once an obscure threat, it has been translated into an object of science, where knowledge itself can bring some relief. But what if this scientific description misses something? What if what makes us ill, in illness, is precisely what is non-scientific, non-technical or non-rational and cannot be so described? What if illness is the opposite of science?

It's perhaps a strange thought that illness isn't scientific, because our custom of describing illness in scientific terms has entrenched itself so much that we have largely forgotten that diabetes or glaucoma is not in itself a scientific but a natural phenomenon. And when we don't use scientific terms we use military ones. Particularly in the case of viruses and cancers, we personify them as if they were a clever, cunning, calculating enemy. Of a cancer we might say that it 'thinks' it's got to reproduce, of a virus that it's 'attacking' the spinal cord and of loved ones that they are 'fighting' an infection. Scientific or military or both, the language we use for illness creates the sense of a rational intelligence at large. But in those very metaphors is the hint of a quite different character. For example, the guerrilla features of the virus that lies dormant before springing up at random point towards a force that is subversive, insurgent and violent; they suggest, rightly, that while illness is capable of being described in rational terms, reason is not its true mode. Why is that?

While it might be rational for a tapeworm, say, to take up residence in the bowel (because as a parasite it has to live off others), we fall ill not because of the tapeworm's behaviour per se, which is rational indeed, but because, when set amidst our own vital needs, that behaviour does us harm. The condition of badness – feeling ill – goes beyond the reasons that caused it. In other words, certain things led up to your falling sick – you picked up the parasite from undercooked meat, say – but the experience of illness puts you in a state that's now not about those causes, but about being sick in its own right. In going beyond its causes, illness passes through the light of reason – the doctor briefly shines her torch on it – and back once more into the dark.

This nocturnal character of illness appears (or disappears) most dramatically in a famous poem by William Blake concerning the rose made sick by a worm of its own:

O Rose, thou art sick!
The invisible worm,
That flies in the night,
In the howling storm,

Has found out thy bed
Of crimson joy;
And his dark secret love
Does thy life destroy.

Ostensibly 'The Sick Rose' is about a canker that affects roses; allegorically, it's about the sickness of human love, and with strong sexual imagery to thicken it. It's contrary, of course, to think of love not as what cures but as what kills – a marauding illness that darkens the door. Having said that, there is a long tradition that portrays love as an affliction, an infirmity which in 'lovesickness' even has a name of its own – referring to the daydreaming, the loss of appetite, the suspension of your rational faculties that occur when you're in love. And if love is a kind of illness, illness is a kind of love, on the grounds that it 'flies in the night', unpredictable and blind like the winged Cupid or a contagion you can't see coming; it gets under your skin and acts itself out in such fevered private rooms as lovers occupy. And, as in love, this essentially febrile aspect of illness can make your mind lose its bearings and wander – if not always to hallucinate, then perchance to dream or fantasise, to pass into the realm of the imagination.

This propensity of illness to express itself in metaphor or imagery is most famously analysed in a book I'll describe in a moment by Elaine Scarry's US contemporary the late Susan Sontag – but first, the most astonishing piece of radio I ever heard. A child psychiatrist was describing a little boy she had treated. What was the presenting symptom? Quite suddenly, at the age of four, the boy's personality changed. Where he had been bright, outgoing, lively and curious, overnight he became withdrawn, morose and uncommunicative; this had gone on for months. Previously the boy's parents had enlisted the help of various medical professionals, but without joy. Now psychiatrist and boy had the following exchange:

> What do you think is wrong with you?
> *Silence.*
> Would you like to tell me what you think it is?
> I can't.
> You can, if you like. I won't be angry.
> You haven't got enough paper.
> *The psychiatrist looks quizzical.*

I've got plenty of paper, look. How much would you like? And I have all these crayons too. Would you like to draw something?

The little boy takes a piece of paper and draws a line from top to bottom; he then takes a second piece and does the same. He puts the two together so that the line continues from one sheet to the next. He takes a third sheet, draws a third line, adds it on to the end of the line on the first two and so on. The boy keeps going until the paper has run out and the floor of the therapist's room is traversed by an uninterrupted line in crayon. 'It was then that I knew,' said the psychiatrist on air, 'that the poor little boy had a tapeworm.'

In the psychiatrist's anecdote, the illness exploits the boy's faculties, in order to appear semi-mystically in imagery, almost as if that boy were the earthly secretary of an unearthly daemon, the mouthpiece of the illness. Even if you don't connect with the somewhat supernatural feeling of the story, it gets at the sensation we often have when we're fed up of hosting an illness that's passing through us, becoming its randomly chosen vehicle. But what Susan Sontag argues in *Illness as Metaphor* is that typically we construe things the other way round: we consider the illness an expression of the person – you are what you get ill from. Rather than addressing illness as a purely physiological phenomenon to be accounted for wholly in terms of aetiology or epidemiology, we entertain all sorts of personality-driven associations between sickness and sufferer that reflect poorly on the latter. That might explain why, when you show up at the doctor's, a part of you will worry that she'll not just assess your symptoms but from them make inferences about your character. Having bad circulation means you're a cold fish, for example – deficient in human warmth; getting cancer means you were always eaten up inside and that which has been repressed gets expressed at last, in the cruellest fashion. Like it or not, your illness tells on you, and we listen to it without knowing it, like people stuck in the sixteenth century who, in the 'theory of the humours', had a prototype version: if, say, your spleen had an excess of black bile, you were a 'melancholic', a word to convey your character as much as your condition. The message is that if you really want to know who someone is, look not into their eyes but into their medical records.

Once you learn that Sontag's book was drafted during the first wave of AIDS (and reprinted as *AIDS and Its Metaphors*), it's not so surprising that she stresses those associative qualities of illness. AIDS was the 'gay disease' which gave the moral majority an excuse to preach the downfall of Sodom; it both exposed the promiscuous character of those contracting it and punished them in kind. Nor should we forget the unfathomable, almost mythical inscrutability of AIDS in those early days: as it swept like Blake's 'invisible worm' out of the dark continent into the West, simply not enough was known about it to neutralise the images it spawned. Nowadays, of course, far more is known, just as far more is known about every disease under the sun, and that expansion in knowledge has produced, one hopes, less reliance on the metaphors Sontag deplored, which were as spiteful as they were specious. Even if a tacit and malevolent law has decreed that there must always be more disease than cure, the conquest of scientific fact over illness-as-mystery continues without impediment, and so your hopes for recovery are never misplaced.

Yet this character-based connection between pain and patient has in the meantime found other lodgings. Even as mainstream medicine surges ahead, it sees itself matched at a distance by the 'alternative medicine' that is its bane, and that reasserts the link not just between different parts of the body but between body and mind, and therefore between suffering and self. When you visit a homoeopath, for example, you're very much taking your whole being along, not just pointing at where it hurts, as you would with a regular medic who's been educated, like a philosopher who believes in the dualism of the body and the mind, to separate mental and physical data. It's precisely in the face of such clinical purity that the alternative, holistic tradition believes body and mind intertwine to form a network of neural and mental pathways: instead of being dragged down by the body, the mind unites with it and together they project a whole that is more advanced than, on its own, either one could ever be. The presumption in this second, less legitimised tradition is of an asset rather than a deficit model, whereby 'medicine' aims at so much more than the medicating of a disorder, or the correcting of a momentary malfunction. A modern branch of ancient Gnosticism, which holds that we all have a god within us just waiting to be let out, it seeks nothing short of the maximisation, the efflorescence, of human potential; in this respect it actively celebrates the power of the body to represent the character and even become the medium of the soul. In theory, you could leave your appointment not just cured but enlightened.

The trouble is that this alternative tradition plays into the hands of the witch doctor, the shaman, the faith healer – all those practitioners who, in place of the reassuring diploma, pot plant and receptionist, accoutre themselves with ethnic arcana, non-specific aromas and hypnotic auras, which serve to mystify the personage of said practitioner even more than the already enigmatic illness. If her authority is built into the relationship with the patient, it doesn't take much for a doctor, even unwittingly, to exploit it, especially when the desperation for a cure can anaesthetise us, the patient, to those who purport to do the curing. What's worse, the mysterious cure might not only not cure us but deal a terrible blow – you visit the acupuncturist to subtly realign your energy and end up with an infection from the needles. Faced with such a prospect, who wouldn't side with the old school, the one that's at least officially sanctioned?

Actually, it's a moot point. Set aside for a moment the question of authority: alternative practitioners may well preach all sorts of mysteries like chi or chakra, but is that any less pompous and self-serving than donning a white coat, deferring to the medical scriptures and codifying ailments in ancient Greek? Both are means of mystifying the doctor's authority, and both, therefore, means of keeping us in awe before them, and making our visit to the doctor such a call on our faith … Even the orthodox tradition has long embraced techniques that confuse the opposition between health and harm. For since at least the discovery of penicillin, the notion of a doctor dispensing apparently noxious substances for beneficial effect has, even in the corridors of medical power, gained credence and forced attention on to what, bar the famous 'placebo effect', is possibly the most mysterious phenomenon of all – that what kills does indeed cure. In fact, long before Fleming's eureka moment of 1928 regarding the curative powers of bacteria, an ambiguity had been signalled in the word '*pharmakon*' in Greek, which translates as *both* poison *and* cure; and the ambiguity carries through into such insalubrious English phrases as 'hair of the dog' – that is, the cure for a hangover being a drink. The counter-intuitive principle, which applies to certain vaccines, is that a little bit of what is bad for you can do you the world of good. The question then is how little is little. For, whatever the mysteries, it seems clear that the human body presents a highly reactive environment, a site where a minimal difference in dosage can produce a maximal difference in results – remedy tipping back over into poison – and where, therefore, the stakes are rarely low. On the other hand, get the prescription right and you will experience what might genuinely be called a modern miracle.

You also hold such miracles in your own hand, and for all the authority of doctors and their institutions, you have a say in getting well too. A moment ago I mentioned the placebo effect and, more than anything else in medicine, this speaks to your potential as a person, to heal thyself – and not through treatment, but belief. For a placebo is the pharmacological form taken by rhetoric, the power of persuasion literally encapsulated. To enter the doctor's surgery is to enter, as we have seen, not only a brightly lit clinical space of reason, rectitude and remedy, but also a shadowy world of authority, imagination and the irrational where our emotions as much as our bodies are in play and our vulnerability rises with each minute spent among the magazines in the waiting room. What you're waiting for in the waiting room is the precious relief that comes with knowledge, making the waiting a kind of blindness. And as our vulnerability rises, so our resistance to persuasion falls, meaning that we become more and more amenable to the effects of the placebo that the doctor may dispense. Which is no bad thing: when we swallow it, we're not just taking her word but also convincing ourselves, and that means we don't, in fact, always need the doctor to supply it. The point of the placebo is that if we believe we'll get better, the chances are we will.

6

Having lunch with your parents

FROM THE MOMENT WHEN, as newborns, we suck on the teat of the breast or bottle she presses to our lips, we connect with our mother through food. In truth, the connection had already formed, via the umbilicus, in the womb, and it continues for as long after weaning as she spoon-feeds her brood, ties them to her apron strings, sends care packages to kids who've flown the coop or gathers the scattered family for a festive lunch. Motherhood and apple pie keep the children going. And the father? His remit as 'provider' plays out nowhere more critically than in his capacity to put food on the table, and in a set of cherished metaphors of his own. Dad is the 'breadwinner' who 'makes the dough' for the 'daily bread', and so, even if it calls for less 'loafing about' and more 'putting his snout in the trough', he is expected to 'bring home the bacon'.

Stereotypes these may be, but however they divvy it up, mum and dad share an essential duty, at least in the formative years, which is to nourish the lives they have sprung from uncreation. Apart from anything else, that's what life is – the drive to sustain itself and thrive – which means that, without food, life is as unviable as it is therefore hard to imagine. Put into the equation the staggering helplessness of human life in its infant state and the responsibility on the parents to compensate for it by providing food dramatically shoots up. Because life depends on food, you've got to feed the lives that depend on you; and if it's by virtue of having children together, of jointly forging new life, that parents become parents, they remain so by keeping that life alive and kicking.

In the schema developed in the mid-twentieth century by psychologist Abraham Maslow, being a parent therefore thrusts you right to the bottom of the 'hierarchy of human needs', a ready reckoner which says you can't get on to more sophisticated things like forming relationships or appreciating works of art – both modes of 'self-actualisation' – before the basics, such as food and shelter, have been sorted. The oceans of love a mother might give her baby can't replace the precious drops of colostrum, so all the talk of love as vital to a baby's needs is somewhat romantic; and nursing mothers, woken in the night for the umpteenth feed, know just how mechanical it can all get, often resenting their new job as 'milk machine'. Even if you twist the hierarchy into a circle by saying that feeding the offspring is itself an act of love and not just a duty, the essential role of the parent can never not include this rudimentary element, and the responsibility to discharge that role of provider is immense.

So paramount is this responsibility to feed and nurture the young lives the parents have created, it alters the value of their own. In life, children come first, relegating their parents to a poor second – which is why the flight attendant's advice to parents to put on their own oxygen masks before those of their children feels so wrong and throws the heart into conflict with the head. Surely one tends to the children before the adults? A parent is one who in prioritising the life of the child will risk his or her own, and as soon as you start making sacrifices for your children, there's no bar on where it might end. How, as a parent, could you ever say you wouldn't give up your own life to save your child? Protecting the child's life is everything, which means the life of the parent ultimately counts for nothing.

That's the first paradox in the otherwise impregnable triangle that yokes together parents, children and food. Without their parents creating them, children can't exist, and once existing, they depend on those parents to keep them in existence with food and water. In this respect, the life of the parent is indispensable to the life of the child. But precisely because parents are obliged to do anything for the sake of the younger life, even to the point of self-sacrifice, the value of their own lives flips over and they now become dispensable to the nth degree. In the interests of the child, the parent signs up to the possibility of being consigned, in the last resort, to death, which means it's in no longer being a parent that the parent's ultimate value cashes out.

The second paradox is that in offering themselves up in sacrifice for their children, the parents themselves become a kind of food. After all, you can't offer up your life without offering up your body – what would that look like? – and so you are, in sacrifice, agreeing to the use or abuse of your body for the satisfaction of someone else, be it god or foe, in an effort to appease them and slake their real or figurative appetite. The most striking and widely practised version of this comes in the Christian Eucharist, of course, whereby worshippers consume the flesh and blood of the Lord, in the form of bread and wine. In this sacrificial trade between parents and children, nothing less than the physical bodies of the parents is at stake, with the implicit offer that they be eaten before the bodies of their children, pacifying thereby the hunger that might otherwise turn on those children first. The parents become the food, and on the triangle the three points collapse into two.

So lunch with your parents may have more meaning than you think. If we've grown accustomed to thinking of meals as rituals, and of family traditions involving eating as warranting anthropological interest, that's just the thin end of the wedge. Even if they appear only on the symbolic level, never to materialise in the dramatic choices hinted at above, the links between parents, children and food run very deep, and the implications can be grave. But as if those paradoxes weren't enough, there is another one, even more heartbreaking, whereby it is not the parents but the children who sacrifice themselves through food. We can get at this through the amazing work of Bert Hellinger, who will describe an extreme case, and then we'll turn to Thomas Malthus, the founder of modern demography, who will help explain why food and sacrifice go together in even the most normal circumstances, and why having lunch with your parents might be such a significant affair.

In a multifaceted career, Hellinger has been a therapist, a priest and a philosopher, and latterly brought all of these fields together in the practice of which he is founding father. Called Constellations, it consists in diagnosing emotional problems in families through having them represented in spatial form. In front of a small group of strangers, with none of the other family there to interfere, one of that family's members – the 'issue-holder' – relays the problem. The 'constellator' agrees with the issue-holder what the elements of the problem are – an ex-wife, two children and a house to divide between them, for example – and these elements are then parcelled out to different people in the room, who will represent them. The issue-holder physically puts each representative into geographical relation with every other representative – he or she will move them into position in the room until the spatial relationship between them mirrors the one in his or her mind's eye. You end up with a living map – the constellation – of what's wrong and where. As a technique it's remarkable enough – if somewhat bizarre – but it is the insights it produces that are the more striking, and most striking among these is that the emotional (and often physical) health of families is influenced, disproportionately and adversely, by members who have been cast out, forgotten or denied. It's not so much that the black sheep of the family will turn up on the doorstep demanding money and making a ruckus, but that, quite unwittingly, one of the white sheep will take on the black sheep's issues and manifest them as an illness or simply a malaise. An alcoholic uncle, the very mention of whose name is verboten, will transplant himself, also unwittingly, into the anaemic nephew who can't seem to get enough blood inside him; the twin given up for adoption will affect the twin who was kept, with an inconsolable loneliness;

and the insomniac who thrashes about in the sheets will have unconsciously absorbed the fate of the grandfather killed in action, who never got a proper burial – for in the emotional algebra of the family, the dead count for as much as the living.

I'll describe one of the many constellations I have seen. A father in his late thirties says he wants help: his fifteen-year-old daughter has stopped eating; her weight has dropped catastrophically and she has been admitted to a psychiatric hospital, where she's not to drink water before being weighed. Nurses monitor her mealtimes at close quarters and she's followed to the bathroom to ensure she doesn't throw the food up, or flush it surreptitiously away. But although the institution has put in place such empirical obstacles to her ruses for the avoidance of food, within her a psychological nihilism runs amok; she's bent on self-destruction. This isn't to say there aren't empirical causes. She is a teenage girl, and teenage girls, already self-conscious about their bodies – a condition known in medical history as a 'ferment in the feminals' – are in all sorts of ways bullied to be thin. She's also an overachiever at a single-sex private school, an 'exam factory' infamous for the anorectic casualties it's produced. If you include the fact that the father himself deserted the roost when the daughter was six, you have what in other situations you might call the 'recipe' – a set of leading indicators – for anorexia nervosa.

But it was to beyond the empirical that the constellation pointed. Like iron filings, the particles of the problem, as embodied by the strangers in the group, angled themselves towards a magnetic north buried not in the daughter but in the father's own death wish. The deeper motive for the girl starving herself to death was to save the father from the death, privately, he had been courting for himself. Affected by suicidal fantasies, his mission was to exclude himself in the most terminal fashion imaginable, and without knowing it, his prescient daughter was making an intervention: she was offering herself up instead. As in *Jude the Obscure*, where, on overhearing his parents' anguish about providing for their children, the oldest hangs himself, the child lands on the final solution. Anorexia does an equally exorbitant, generous and misguided bit of arithmetic: if food be a resource that is both essential for life but finite, better that the parent take it. In this and other ways, parents and children wrestle to put each other first, and food becomes their primary arena.

This anxiety over resources within the family doesn't require a constellation to stage it, of course, and there are less earnest ways of approaching the subject altogether – Jonathan Swift's famous satire, *A Modest Proposal*, recommended feeding on children as an answer to the Irish famine of the eighteenth century. Because the tone is so well sustained, you have to read on quite a bit before you realise that Swift isn't being serious. And there are still different approaches to this triangular relationship between parents, children and food, the most famous perhaps being that of Malthus in the early nineteenth century, which construed it as a matter for demographic analysis. In simple terms, the size of the family is determined by the amount of food available, though that doesn't necessarily mean that rich people have more children – it usually works the other way round, for reasons we'll see. What's constant is the desire of populations to increase themselves, for if the first principle of life is to sustain itself, the second is to procreate, which puts pressure in turn on the resources available for sustenance. The result is a stop-and-go motion over time, the modern analogy for which might be traffic patterns before a bottleneck: each car goes as fast as it can until forced to slow down by all the others doing the same, and a lurching fast-slow movement, rather than a steady 40 mph, becomes the rhythm. In Malthus's words, the drive to reproduce 'increases the number of people before the means of subsistence are increased'.

The consequences are far-reaching. Because populations want to increase themselves, they veer into and out of alignment with the resources they need. What's more, they tend to increase *before*, not after, the extra food required appears. That is the macro picture, but it controls the individual family at the micro level: who will make what might appear to be irrational choices about how many children it can support, or how far any such children might eventually support the family. For if populations increase before the necessary resources become available, this means it's precisely when they're unsure how they're going to feed it that parents are more, rather than less, likely to have another child – hence the issue of sacrifice, of potentially having to give away a child who is too expensive to feed at home. One interpretation for this 'irrational' expansion of the family is that, as times of hunger approach, it's building the family's capacity for the future that outweighs providing for it in the present – the more children you have, the greater the opportunity for finding or generating resources for the family, even if this carries the risk of future sacrifice when those resources fail to materialise. Which would also explain that parallel, if perverse, truth that wealthier societies have fewer children, and also shows how primal, in what Malthus calls 'seasons of distress', is the vital urge for more life: if it looks as if the species is going to die out, we start to reproduce and life prepares to take its chances.

When you sit down for lunch with your parents, humdrum as it is, you might want to acknowledge the minor miracle it enshrines. They gave you life and fed you, and you're breaking bread with them in memory of the fact that the family extended itself, in both senses, to accommodate you, also in both senses: your very life came to pass in the hope that sharing the meal might be possible. And yet many people experience it quite differently, or even feel the reverse. Rather than nestling into the bosom of the family and allowing their worries to melt away, they anticipate the parental lunch with something closer to dread. A passing knowledge of family psychology informs them that a portion of their own woes can be laid at their parents' door and their anger is piqued: in the words of Philip Larkin, 'They fuck you up, your mum and dad.'

You can't choose your parents, and you didn't ask to be born (technically impossible, of course), but there you are, fucked up by these weird people you might otherwise never give the time of day; you can't even undo the association with them because it thrums in your blood. There's no getting round the entanglement, and if it rarely prompts active vengeance on the parents by their children, it commonly causes acute embarrassment – which suggests that embarrassment can be defined as a crisis of belonging: it's when I'm associated with something I don't associate myself with, that that same blood wells up through the neck. Dad makes a racist remark over the roast chicken, Mum hoists the blind in the kitchen to gawp at the neighbours, and the grown-up child is pitched into an agony of conscience. The meal rebinds the family with a force that for some is like a straitjacket, because they cannot reconcile their belonging to their family with the life they have established for themselves; or, as fully fledged adults, they can't bear to be reminded that they were children once – here they are again being fattened in the family home – nor that their independence has stemmed from its polar opposite.

Of course, lunch with the parents is as likely to take place in a restaurant, and for children who have grown up and made their own lives, the whole scene comes to a head with the paying of the bill. The relationship with your parents will probably pass through three broad phases: first comes your dependency on them, last comes their dependency on you, and in the middle falls a period of transition, with the uncertainty that implies (not that phases one and two don't come with challenges of their own). If you're out to lunch with your parents, it's probably happening in this interregnum during which who's in charge, and therefore who pays, is not self-evident. Yes, you're earning now, but these are your *parents*: even if you're lucky enough that your monthly take-home doubles their life savings, the idea of buying them lunch also has the smell of something running contrary to what nature intended and so there might, before opening your wallet, be good reason to pause. On the other hand, even if you're as poor as a church mouse, isn't it nice to be able to pay, to chuck some modest lump into the vast crater of debt to your parents that, as their child, you find yourself standing in? They haven't just fed you, they've sheltered you, kept you clean, bought you clothes, seen to your education and performed the bulk of the functions that have fashioned the very conscience with which you make your judgement over whether to cough up. So where on the table ought the waiter to place the bill?

Nearest the parent, as a sign of respect? Closer to the adult child, in recognition that the times are changing? Or, diplomatically, halfway between the two?

Actually, Bert Hellinger would read the question as futile. The debt we owe our parents can never be squared, and jolly good too, because doing so would threaten to nullify all relationship, all emotional commerce between the two generations. Being in debt, just like being in credit, means an active interest applies between the two parties and, once the debt is taken care of, the interest is bound to wane – settling a debt means closing off the need for relationship, just like when you pay for something in a shop and are free to walk away and never return (you could argue that all relationships depend on being variously in credit or debit – owing a friend a favour or being owed, for example). In this sense, it's better not to try to pay your parents back at all; doing so is almost a denial or perversion of the generational character of that bond. Yes, they gave you life and fed you, but the best form of gratitude is not repayment – it's acceptance. And should you go on and have children of your own, you will in any case pay your parents back by looking after their grandchildren, and keeping life alive. So let your parents pick up the tab; you'll do the same for your own kids when the time comes.

7

Bunking off

JOHN STUART MILL had a famously peculiar upbringing. A child of the revolution whose spirit was drifting across the nineteenth-century Europe he grew up in, he was, from the tenderest age, home-schooled with Horace and hot-housed with Homer. At seven, he had Herodotus by heart. Was it all that early discipline that later turned him into such a champion of freedom? All that being closeted with the classics that made him come out for modern values? Who knows. Whatever its origins, *On Liberty*, the work for which Mill is most fêted, takes great pains to promote the freedom of the individual: individual freedom is what makes life worth living, and society should back off to let it breathe.

If bunking off had a patron saint, then for this, his eulogy to emancipation, Mill might justly be canonised. What kind of an icon would he make? Obviously, nothing like that of the conventional martyr, all rigid with devotion, but something altogether more insouciant and empowered. He might even be represented by an absence, a cartoon of an abandoned desk, perhaps, with the door still swinging to show how blithely he has tripped off into the hills glimpsed beyond; and – in a variation of the ruse hit upon by George Costanza in *Seinfeld*, who leaves his car in the company lot for days on end, but sidles off early to catch the train – on the back of the chair, a jacket left hanging, to fool his colleagues into thinking he's not so flagrantly skipped out for the afternoon.

But why even leave the jacket? Doesn't having to pretend you're still at work mean that the yoke of empowerment's very opposite – enslavement – still hangs around your neck? Does it not suggest that yours might be freedom of an inferior kind? If you're as free as you claim, you should just get up and walk out; and if anyone blocks you, you might impress on them, lest it be mistaken for turpitude, the nobility of your action. For, as long as you're not harming anyone, then slipping away to do a bit of shopping, or hit some balls at the driving range, or rough out a novel, carries no shame. On the contrary, for daring to live out the precepts sanctified by a figure no less than J. S. Mill, you might even expect approbation. Let others, if they must, call it bunking off; to you, it's less about slinking into the shadows than diving into the cold stream of self-determination.

'As long as you're not harming anyone': so there is a fly in the suntan lotion. Go ahead, be free and find yourself, but don't put anyone's nose out of joint in the process – such is the 'harm principle' that Mill attached as the one guy rope to that otherwise unfettered hot-air balloon of Victorian liberty. The grand expedition that is individual freedom can never completely slip its moorings, never quite take off in a loop-the-loop of solipsism and self-delight, because others, boringly, must be taken into account. Which might sound like a moral point, a sediment of Victorian sanctimony that Mill failed to dissolve, but it's more basic than that, for individual liberty doesn't actually work without its sister concept of harm. Why? If liberty is the absence of constraint, and it's only you that has it, then everybody else has to get out of your way, to de-constrain your environment and free up the space for you to expand into your destiny; liberty for you means deference for the hoi polloi, and creates an autocracy where the freedom of one depends on the slavery of all. So the harm principle acts as a circuit breaker, a mechanism that switches the liberty of the individual into the liberty of individuals – not slavery, but freedom for all. If there's a moral, it's that you can skate around the rink to your heart's content – just don't knock anybody over.

Still, to the bunker off, that sounds like a good deal: if you're not actively doing harm to anyone back at the office, you can bunk off with a clear conscience ... Or can you? Unless you plan on paying back the income you'll continue to earn as you swan off to the nail bar, or on working the extra shift to make up for it, you are – not to be too punctilious – violating your contract of employment, and that is tant-amount to causing harm to your employer. Even if it's quiet at work and no one's obliged to cover for you, you're breaking the promise that contract had codified, so either way, financial or symbolic, some damage will be done. It may fall short of the illegal – it's more a minor indulgence or mere peccadillo – but bunking off nevertheless flouts the principle Mill enshrined: in his system, harm can result as much from neglect as action.

Suddenly, freedom looks rather taxing. What, through the window of individual liberty, appeared at first like wide pastures of self-expression now shrinks to a fenced-in backyard, as the harm prin-ciple looms at the gate like a dyspeptic policeman to curb your enthu-siasm. Bunking off starts to look less like fun than like an exercise in ethics. After all, once you start legislating against the unintended con-sequences of your actions, where does it end? While certain cases of indirect harm, like passive smoking, are easy to admit, others are more obscure. It's hard these days to buy new shoes, for example, without a pang for the cheap labour that's gone into them, but exactly how responsible are we? Could it be that every single action you take in your own interest has an equal and opposite impact on someone else? If so, this pesky principle of harm is enough, as you plan to slope off for the afternoon, to take the spring right out of your step.

Not to be discouraged, however, you have at least two ways of letting out the corset on freedom that Mill describes. In answer to the point about harming your employer, for example, a crude riposte says that bunking off constitutes a form of justice, of redressing the imbal-ance between the disgusting amounts the fat cats feed themselves and the crumbs they toss you from their well-appointed table. Being paid to wander off in the middle of the day for an ice cream or romantic tryst or theatre matinée is, all things considered, only fair.

The subtler response says the trade-off between one man's freedom and another man's harm is no trade-off at all. It's not axiomatic that the aggregate of individual freedoms must sum to 100 per cent of freedom available, for it might be in the uniqueness, and therefore the non-comparability, of those freedoms that their individuality lies. In other words, to be truly free and truly individual, each freedom will be infinite, spared from competing with others for room inside the tent of happiness. It isn't a *thing*, freedom, an object that takes up space, so to conceive it as anything other than intangible and subjective amounts to an error; and because it's subjective, the sphere of freedom is not the market but the mind, an inner world which might be a thousand times more fertile than any on the earth's contestable crust. Because one man's freedom is not another man's freedom, harm shouldn't come into it; and where two freedoms do clash, thus stirring the prospect of harm into motion, it means neither was unique or original enough to count as a real freedom in the first place.

Besides, there is a higher medal. While the marriage of freedom and individuality is consummate, it's not the end of the story: their union has to serve the ideal of happiness. After all, if individual freedom led to misery, what would be the point? If bunking off made you feel bad, why bother? So innovative in so many respects, Mill's thinking on this point sits comfortably within a tradition, one established a good two millennia ago by Aristotle and others dedicated to defining what happiness – or what Aristotle preferred to call the good life – might be. Not that this diminishes Mill's standing, and while they converge on 'the good life' as an end, Mill and Aristotle diverge drastically on means. For the moral deregulation favoured by Mill includes, along with the freedom to pursue happiness, the right to judge whether you've found it; in simple terms, only you can say if you're happy. This may not sound so problematic – if anything, it's rather grown up – but it implies that happiness is something you could think yourself into. Since you've only got yourself to judge you, you can set the bar wherever you like; and with no objective definition of happiness to rein you in, any old rubbish could pass muster. Others might pity you for having to bunk off rather than taking pleasure in your job, but so what – you've found some momentary happiness that works for you. And that, one might argue, is no bad thing. If happiness is the final frontier of fulfilment, why not take it where you can get it?

But Aristotle would have been horrified. Set aside the fact that there's the patent risk of self-deception – just because you think you're happy, it doesn't mean you are. Forget too that there's the risk of actual deception, where you end up like Jim Carrey's character in *The Truman Show*, who, while remotely controlled by TV executives broadcasting it for the amusement of others, believed his to be the good life's amplest expression. What's truly misplaced is Mill's trust in the individual to make a judgement about their happiness midstream, for Aristotle insisted on assessing the quality of a life only posthumously, once the whole could be viewed; and, if posthumously, only by others. Like sainthood, the status of 'good life' was something to be given but not assumed, and only in hindsight – or, to continue the film metaphor, the good life simply won't show up in a still, you need to see the entire reel. Apply all that to bunking off – a few hours snatched from the working day, in which you believe you're living the life of Riley – and you can see why the happiness it brings might not count for much at all.

It's not just the ancients who might have been dubious about Mill's theory, and even a successor, like Émile Durkheim, beamed upon it implicit doubt. For Durkheim, individual freedom was precisely what could undermine happiness and even sanity. Not least because it can lead to excessive introspection, individuality was perfidious, and so bunking off could mean jeopardising your well-being. If you'd agreed it with your boss, it would be something different, something sanctioned, but by definition you haven't, and so bunking off is an initiative that's necessarily unofficial, an act that in some small way separates you from society. Of course, it's just such unofficialness that both underwrites its freeness and adds to its thrill, but, as in drug addiction, the first, intoxicating hit of freedom gives way to dependency, and bunking off can rapidly deteriorate into wandering the streets in search of harder-to-reach highs. That infinity which freedom conjures up, once so exhilarating, can reappear as a landscape most forlorn, for the private journey to the bottom of the mind takes with it no companions. 'Liberty' marks not only the apex of individualism but also the origin of madness, and Durkheim was quick to spot the mental side effects of spending too much time alone, going so far as to suggest it underlay phenomena as dolorous as suicide, which all too often represented the surplus of individual liberty over social norms – tendencies towards self-harm being a symptom of alienation. For individual liberty does indeed imply a separation from others which, if the spring of creativity in Mill, was for some of his modernist inheritors the well of loneliness.

So what is the difference between freedom and alienation, bunking off and opting out? To the Durkheimian, very little. When it came to alienation, or what he preferred to call 'anomie', Durkheim was convinced that such shiftlessness – moral isolation, in effect – was caused by an absence of conventions and a rejection of the society that instituted them. To combat this parlous state, his was a remedy to fit with a whole school of thought that is about, well, school. Reading Durkheim is like reading a headmaster, a wholesome type dedicated to the eradication of bunking off and committed to the cataloguing of every breach – not out of fanatical disciplinarianism, but the better to understand how to bring lost sheep back into the fold. Unsurprisingly, the answer was school itself or its equivalents – a spell of peer bonding to promote mutual belonging and a clear set of rules to wall off the ambiguities and anxieties that freedom brings. This places Durkheim in the company of social reformers as diverse as Will Keith Kellogg, conceiver of the corn flake, and Mies van der Rohe, builder of the Bauhaus, both of whom founded institutions on a mission to integrate the individual within a collective plan where its energies could be rationally ordered, and to avoid social disintegration. Bunking off from work, as with playing truant from school, might glitter like a delicious voyage across your individual liberty, but it's not good for your health, and you're better off putting yourself in the hands of well-regulated social institutions, such as schools, bureaucracies and even prisons, designed to stave off the nightmare of being alone, anomic and adrift. By de-priving you of your privateness, emptying your inner thoughts out into the public square, they save you from implosion; and by dismantling the barrier between you and society, thus assimilating you into one larger whole, they remove the opportunity, and with it the desire, for bunking off.

As commendable as it is joyless, Durkheim's model would therefore have a particular intolerance for an essential part of bunking off – its wonderful goallessness. Even Mill's paean to individual freedom, apparently so releasing, assumes a high-minded striving towards a goal, which threatens to make the prosecution of your freedom a kind of work, just as a 'pursuit' of happiness can suggest an easily thwarted, and therefore less than happy, task. Like other pleasures, liberty can become a labour. Yet what is so potent, and potentially subversive, in bunking off is that we might do it without any end, or purpose, in view. After all, if you're bunking off from *work*, from one set of objectives you've been asked to meet, the last thing you want is to replace them with another. Say you skive off to buy new jeans: you've not so much set yourself a goal as constructed a fantasy; but if, three hours later, you're leaving yet another store, tired and empty-handed, only to enter, with ebbing hopes, the store next door, that fantasy will have evaporated like a castle in the air and rebuilt itself as a concrete errand, a chore hardly less enervating than doing the filing you took the afternoon off to avoid. To bunking off there is, in other words, an art, which lies in keeping airborne the spirit that dared you to sneak out in the first place, and that means recreating the conditions of child's play.

Easier said than done, of course: declaring there's an art to bunking off is about as helpful as saying you've got to work at playing – or, as John Stuart Mill himself put it, 'Those only are happy who have their minds fixed on some object other than their own happiness ...' The more self-conscious, the less play-like play becomes, for play is nothing if not the suspension of self-consciousness, the relief from being held to account by the world. What's curious is that this state of suspension merges, in play, with its opposite – complete absorption. The former is even the condition of the latter. By excusing you from the world, play allows for deeper engagement in it, the analogy for which might be looking through a microscope: with one eye closed and peripheral activity blacked out, you slide into a tiny but magnified micro-mega universe where everything makes sense in its own terms, even if those terms bear scant relation to the world outside; your concentration is intense, without being strained; and the distinction between you and what you're observing starts to dissolve. Bunking off should aspire to the same quality of enchantment, and when it achieves this, it becomes one of the few adult forms of play.

In this sense, bunking off, despite what Durkheim might imply, can be good for you – it gifts you with a magic moment, a poem amidst your working day's prose. And for Donald Winnicott, the English psychoanalyst, such experiences are fundamental to your growth as a person. Play, for Winnicott, was a serious matter, a way of negotiating the space between yourself and the world, and he studied countless children as they played with toys that represented both their inner fantasies and the external realities they were learning to contend with. For example, a little girl will use a doll to act out her own growing responsibilities – having to eat up her food or have her nappy changed – while also taking that same doll on a magical mystery tour in a miniature pram, on a route that will have a surreal logic of its own. The doll becomes what Winnicott calls a 'transitional object' that furnishes the little girl with a channel between fantasy and reality. What's crucial to emotional development is getting the balance right – appreciating objective reality and its exigencies, while allowing enough of your own subjective creativity to have its day. Bunking off strikes that balance: because it's an escape from work, you're all too conscious of the rules you're breaking, and so it functions, even as you try to forget them, as a reminder of your social obligations; but because it's also an escape into yourself, it's a time for exploration, for drifting from the norm and inventing possibilities you might otherwise, back at your desk, become inured to. If only by refreshing the repertoire of images in your mind, bunking off unlocks this playful, childlike self that's more akin to the adventurer you always wanted to be than to the employee you became.

There's also a more subtle dynamic in operation. Winnicott, like Freud before and Derrida after him, became fascinated with a simple game in which an infant takes a bobbin – a kind of spool – and rolls it to and fro. In psychoanalytic literature, it's known as the 'Fort-Da', or 'There-Here', a term that echoes the child's commentary on the object as it unfurls ('fort!') and returns ('da!'). That literature claims the bobbin represents the child's mother (who in this case was no less than Freud's own daughter, meaning the child was his grandson, Ernst). The boy is staging the mother's departure and return, in order to come to terms with events that are, in the universe of the child, potentially cataclysmic – for when mummy goes out, the child has no concept of her returning and so the most terrible separation anxiety sets in. But by reproducing that potential trauma, this mini drama, directed by the child, can assuage it. So how does this simple-complex game relate to bunking off?

Well, in bunking off you might be playing a similar game, but instead of thinking about a parent, you are thinking about your boss – and actually representing him. You'd be acting out the boss's own freedom as you perceive it, his own capacity to bugger off for long lunches with impunity, his own unassailable relationship to the business that permits him to get in as late as he pleases, or stay out at what he claims are interminable meetings. By acting the boss, you protect yourself from him, putting yourself in an inviolable position that will neutralise any trauma coming your way. But at the same time, because you only ever bunk off *from* something, you're tied to what you've left behind: it's you who's on a string invisibly attached to work, where work – and especially that arrogant boss – has all the authority of a parent. The freedom of bunking off is at best temporary, at worse phoney, because the umbilical cord remains uncut: you haven't actually quit your job, you've just simulated the feeling of freedom, as if you had. Bunking off means you're playing at sending yourself away ('fort!'), while staying indissolubly connected ('da!').

Bunking off, in other words, sits on a paradox in which you are parent and child at the same time. In so far as you are taking your freedom into your own hands, you are the parent, the adult prepared to run risks, to make a statement and earn the respect of a John Stuart Mill. But in so far as it's sneaky and dependent, bunking off positions you as a child who desperately needs the structure you've briefly deserted. It's a paradox paralleled in the emotions felt in the moment: on the one hand, the high self-esteem of the bunker off that says you're too important for all the crap that goes with being at work; on the other hand, the self-deprecation that concedes nothing will be adversely affected if you take the afternoon off, which means you're not so important after all. As an activity, bunking off will always be ambivalent, a strange mixture of freedom and constraint. That said, on your deathbed it won't be the extra hours working through your in-tray that you'll remember.

8

Shopping

IN DOWNTOWN DUBAI, where the average daytime temperature tops 30 Celsius or 86 Fahrenheit, you can, within a glass dome within a certain mall, and flanked by stores the likes of Adidas, Louis Vuitton and Paul Smith, go skiing. Complete with cable cars and conifers, the world's most unlikely indoor ski slope welcomes humid hordes hourly to a perpetual winter amid the searing crucible of the Arabian dunes, as miraculous as an oasis whose water has frozen like sorbet beneath a burning shell. As the words themselves have been trying to tell us for ages, dessert and desert are not so far apart.

Impressive though the Gulf State's trick of temperatures may be, all the snowdome has done is turn down further the dial in the mall's already air-conditioned atmosphere. The apparition of snow-under-sun only extends an artificiality the mall had long boasted and so is not a genuine innovation but, quite literally, a matter of degree. For it was in defiance of nature that the mall was conceived, scouting out the least hospitable location – no water supply, no roads, not even an indigenous customer base – and pitching its tent. Once there, however, it flourished. Which means the mall's real innovation lay in discovering, just when we thought we'd got them wrapped up, a new law of psychology: build it and they will come. In the Islamic kingdom of Dubai, it's what makes Mohammed come to the mountain – one with real snow.

In this respect, the mall embodies the soul of the frontier, Dubai the kin of California. Colonising the wild, it 'took dominion everywhere', to quote 'Anecdote of the Jar', the poetic parable, set in another US state, of Wallace Stevens:

> I placed a jar in Tennessee,
> And round it was, upon a hill.
> It made the slovenly wilderness
> Surround that hill.

For jar, read mall: though built of glass and air, the immaterial matter of reflection, the mall makes everything else surround it. It glitters above the 'slovenly wilderness' from which its patrons will have trekked, mesmerised by what it has to offer. Despite or because of its vacuity, the domed mall, like the round jar, is replete with dreams, and both emit scintillas of light which crystallise into an image of the future to dazzle all around.

In other respects, the mall is not empty, but the reverse. It's an emporium, a souk, stocked with continuously replenished product lines; stuffed with stuff, it is the very spirit of materialism. Don't be fooled, however, that the mall is therefore just a new, improved market, continuing in the vein of the good old 'supermarket' or even its big brother, the 'hypermarket'. While the mall celebrates the market in the abstract sense of free-market capitalism, it despises the literal, homespun market of goods and stalls it so magisterially supersedes. Besides scale, three aspects mark the mall out from its humble predecessor:

1. You can call the mall artificial and it will take it as a compliment. For the mall has redefined 'artificial' as no longer inferior to 'natural', the latter being the value to which the market in town most clings. Nor any longer is what's 'artificial' the imperfect imitation of nature – for the artificiality of the mall actually comes closer to perfection, its controlled environment not just a shopper's paradise but possibly heaven itself. Isn't such hubris bound, you

may wonder, to incur the wrath of God? When we go to the mall, we are saying that it doesn't matter; we just got tired of waiting for heaven, so we went ahead and built it.

2. The mall despises the market in town, not only because of that clean-cut contempt for country manners, but because while the market – setting up stall in the forum, the square, the piazza where the merry folk gather to barter and banter – encourages exchange of all kinds, the mall insists on depersonalised transaction. Customers are permitted to pass their credit card to the cashier with the semi-automatic smile, but God forbid they should mingle with each other.

3. The market has cash as its king, but put him in the mall and the king becomes a leper whom the mall will barely countenance, unable to compute or scan this throwback to a world where goods and their value were so directly linked. In the mall, the credit card reigns, and imposes a quite different economics, in which the financial value pumped from credit card to till becomes almost superfluous to its value-added, which lies in the information leaked by the card about its holder. If the credit card has become the essential tool of modern shopping, it's because it encodes the identity you are noiselessly trading in return for those new shoes, where identity has become the commodity considered most priceless of all. Like a form of DNA, your credit card transactions leave traces that make patterns that make a proxy of your personality; whereas the very filthiness of cash is what allows it to be laundered and the dirty marks that track back to your identity may be sponged away.

Just as credit cards evince an evolution from cash, so shopping signals an advance from the crude activity of buying: where buying is reducible to an exchange, shopping adds up to an experience. But like other verbs that began life as a noun (parenting, for example), shopping, though based on the end-stopped, no-nonsense, Anglo-Saxon '*shop*', has never become transitive enough, never an active verb ('buying', by contrast, arrived well before its noun – as in 'that car was a good buy'). Let's remember you can still go shopping without buying, because where buying is a matter of need, shopping is a question of want: yes, the more bags you go home with the more gratified you'll be, but even if you return with the trunk of your Toyota as unencumbered as on the day you bought it, you can still say you've been shopping – for a good couple of hours you've been in a state of drawn-out wanting, and that counts. Shopping numbs the senses, and as you ride the myriad escalators that caterpillar through its halls, it's clear you've given yourself over to a vast machine. Try as it might to fit itself around the customer, the customer had long before signed up to fitting around the mall (the jar, again), which means that rather than having to think about what you might need, you'll abandon yourself to the disembodied voices both detailing and retailing what you want. From the mall's perspective, your acquiescence is almost as good as your acquisitiveness.

This sense in the mall's pleasure-dome of unreality, or hyper-reality, or what you might call '*mall du siècle*' ('shopping sickness'), has been analysed at length by academics. What's been less discussed is what underwrites it, which is credit itself – not money as such, but trust and confidence, both of which are not only abstract but guaranteed by the future. 'Credit' comes from the Latin '*credere*', 'to believe', for credit is the belief that the money you're borrowing will someday be returned, a belief that needs the future to function in. After all, once the very desert has been annexed for footfall, space runs out and there's nowhere to go but time, the only time available being what's still to come. Without credit, shopping – as opposed to buying – is inconceivable, for shopping was always about the future, about the better life them folk from the wilderness dreamed of. Like ticket and barrier in the mall's car park, deferral and belief go together: you haven't paid yet for your ticket, but, in the belief that you will, the barrier rises to let you in.

This deferral has psychological, as well as economic, characteristics. The psyche will do anything to avoid pain, and when faced with something traumatic, like having to pay, its instinct is to put it off

– what Freud called 'Nachträglichkeit' or delayed effect. Credit card and psyche conspire to soften the blow of paying by staggering it over time. But it still comes at a price, which on the credit card statement is an accrual of interest, and in the psyche is a build-up of that denied truth, forming a sediment called the unconscious. Sooner or later, both will come back to haunt you – so never say the never-never never returns. Yet although the pain of payment can't be avoided for ever, in the short term its deferral can even feel like pleasure. This is the first reason why retail is therapeutic: it takes something potentially taxing (parting with money) and, by manipulating the terms so that you pay nothing until next year, converts it all into an upside with no pressing downside. The implication, paradoxically, is that it's better to be faced with a pain and have it temporarily subdued than carry on as you were. The second reason is that, because of its simultaneous pushing back of economic reality and bringing forward of gifts, shopping makes a child of you. Psychoanalytically speaking, shopping is a restaging of the scene in which mummy and daddy, while sheltering you from the financial frosts encircling the house, station themselves by the hearth and give you presents as tokens of their love.

As the ad put it so well, it's because you're worth it. In the products you shop for, you are seeking the reflection of yourself as this deserving, loved object, which suggests your true aim is to create a positive image of yourself. Effectively, that makes shopping a form of narcissism – a phenomenon that's often understood to mean just 'vanity', but with other interesting aspects that apply to shopping. Narcissus, of course, was the gorgeous Greek youth described by Ovid who, in crouching over a stream 'with shiny, silvery waters', fell in love with his own reflection, and for Jacques Lacan, the psychoanalyst, it is the mirroring itself, as much as the self-love, that matters. Lacan homes in on a pivotal moment, an epiphany when, in early childhood, the infant looks in the mirror and first realises he is a whole being. Until this *coup de foudre* or lightning bolt, the little one has not apprehended his own oneness, for all has been disconnected sensation without a centred self to anchor it. It's as if, after years of sitting dumbly at a parade of TV images, he finds the remote: the self becomes the console of integration and he sees that everything comes together in himself.

But with this substantial gain comes significant loss, and it reminds us why the story of Narcissus is not comic but tragic. If Narcissus fell in love with himself, it was because of a curse placed on him by Echo, the nymph who repeated everybody's words. Why a curse? Out of revenge, Echo wanted young Narcissus to taste the bitterness of unrequited love that he had made her suffer, and so fixed it that whenever he reached into the pool to touch the face that so entranced him, it shattered into watery splinters: 'How often did he vainly kiss the treacherous pool, how often plunge his arm deep in the waters as he tried to clasp the neck he saw! But he could not lay hold upon himself.' Apart from the fact that Ovid's Narcissus doesn't realise it's himself that he's grasping for, the text describes well the agony of post-mirror-stage development in Lacan. You now have an identity that you can see but cannot touch; you know you are a whole self because the mirror says so, but you never quite feel it. Slipping on that designer jacket, the image you've created remains beyond your grasp.

Such is the price we pay as we try on clothes in the fitting room, with its slimming mirrors and flattering lighting, all designed to close the gap between you and your image. Yet shops will do whatever they can to make you feel as if you might become integrated with yourself once more. They thrust at you all the tools you'll ever need to assemble an identity, precisely to negate the narcissistic hex of being separated from the self that you can see, and help you experience yourself as a coherent whole from which you may indeed derive some vain pleasure. The shop does its utmost to welcome you inside the mirror, to overcome the division between the two dimensions, and make you look and feel your best all of the time, such that 'best' becomes the norm.

In fact, the entire shopping mall could be seen as the transfiguring of this world into that more luminous land on the other side of the mirror, and this is emphasised by the building's physical transparency, the whole topped with a glass roof and all public space formalised into the obligatory atrium. Simply by keeping the weather out, letting light in and maintaining a perfect cleanliness, the atrium interprets the shoppers to be as ideal as the figurines who foreshadowed them in the architect's studio. But it wasn't always that way: although the vitreous spaces of today's mall are transparent to the point of suggesting permeability, its earlier, more classic versions – that is, the shop window – continued to erect a barrier, against which one might press one's nose (something that in the mall would be frowned upon). When shops were mainly in, not out of, town, and not as decisively divorced from their origins in the market, they created a very different idea of the self, one most famously compressed into the figure that Walter Benjamin, who had a mind like a magpie, appropriated from Baudelaire and others, of the 'flâneur'. Who he?

In Benjamin's words, the flâneur 'is the observer of the market place', strolling through its arcades, particularly those of Paris – 'capital of the nineteenth century' – and past its shop fronts. The leisurely pace of his perambulation speaks to the flâneur's detachment, self-satisfaction and culpability, the three cocktail ingredients of decadence. In this the flâneur is the ultimate bourgeois, suffused with his own smugness, but although this compromises him politically, philosophically he is in Benjamin's eyes fascinating, the missing link between the grand narrative of history and the incidents of daily life. The discontinuity of his sensations as he passes from shop to shop tells a truth about the modern world, the way that rather than describing an arc it gushes into rockpools of time, brief and brilliant moments that, like a Monet painting, seen up close are incoherent, but when you step back resolve into a tableau. Or they don't resolve at all, even at a distance, and are left, more like a Miró than a Monet, in a relationship to each other that is at best latent. And that might cause us to reflect upon reflection: unlike the postmodern poseur's superpenetration into the mirror of the mall, the flâneur must deal with the semi-opaque shop window, in which the image of himself gets confused with the items displayed inside, his face ghoulishly floating at an undefined focal length. The self is even more elusive than it was for Narcissus: the reflective surface of the shop window, unlike the silvered water of the pool, couldn't produce a reliable enough picture of the thing – the self – that you're supposed to want. This has the effect, not unuseful, of limiting the desire for it and making you less grasping – perhaps heading for the high street rather than the mall is better for your soul.

And if it's hard to see yourself in the shop window, it's also because, being on the street where kids and carts pass by, rather than under the vast hygienic awning of the mall, its glass gets smeared. In French, the words for window-shopping are *'lèche vitrine'*, which transliterate as 'lick window' (hence the suitably sensuous track by Aphex Twin called 'Windowlicker') and has a wonderful salaciousness, evoking the shop-front smudges of classic shopping. Without wishing to get too nostalgic about it, this was an era when the relationship with the shop involved something tactile – if not always the use of tongues, at least the use of hands – where you'd squeeze the fruit or stroke the cloth before buying, an era superseded by that of 'just looking', and sales assistants who swoop to refold the sweater should you dare disturb it on the shelf. Today you can indeed go shopping and just look – for the eyes have it.

One thought before closing: about opening times. The other difference between the old shop, which invites curiosity, and the new mall, which controls and channels it, is that the shop had a shorter, and clearly posted, set of hours. The mall, by contrast, may well be open for business practically round the clock, which means it not only finds another way of defying the laws of nature, it has also gone a long way towards positioning itself in cyberspace. Part of the reason for establishing itself in remote geographies is to attempt leaving the physical landscape altogether. And once unhinged from space, it becomes detached from time as well: there's so much time that it disappears, making going to the mall hardly different from logging on. Rather than competing with the Internet, in other words, the mall nearly reproduces it, the store assistants consulting the company's own website in order to assist. And if it reproduces the Internet, the mall's operating in a universal time zone makes it indistinguishable from the airport lounge too. It deregulates the rhythm of the day, so that you can eat breakfast all day and purchase pearls at midnight. And just as it deregulates the day, so it liberates the seasons and even in high summer you can go downhill skiing.

9

Booking a holiday

AN ANTIDOTE TO THE AUSTERE, holidays should aim at the luxurious – opulence, not oppression; spa, not spartan. No sooner is the holiday proposed than a throng of seductive images gathers round to oil its back: the 'unspoilt' beach, the 'turquoise' sea, the 'secluded' resort, the 'tranquil' bay … and if all that sounds too recumbent, it usually comes with a kick, like village moonshine, of 'local colour'. Even if we've come to realise that local colour might mean cockroach-infested restaurants, barefoot kids pestering you with tat or meat-market discos on potholed roads that peter out before the electricity substation, still the fantasy holds. The holiday is halcyon.

Apart from anything else, this resilience of our holiday fantasies proves their allure is, to a not insignificant degree, linguistic. If we avert our eyes from the beggar waving her stump to 'lose ourselves' in the 'ancient' alleys of the 'exotic' spice market, it's partly because the holiday brochures withhold language for the unsightly. No sooner do we arrive than we hunt for the reality that corresponds to the descriptions we've read; and when the two, language and reality, coincide – the words 'powdery white sand' with the spongy stuff subsiding beneath our soles – joy breaks out. We see what the advertisements have corrected our vision to see and, having clocked it, we reproduce it ourselves, by writing postcards about that powdery sand, or photographing the palm tree against the sunset, or taking home the piece of indigo silk like the one in the guidebook. And so the whole thing turns in a self-perpetuating cycle. Holidays take place as much in language as in locations, and it's what they get much of their luxuriousness from. The tightly bound lexicon of travel plants itself in front of any reality that might contradict it, protecting you like a tour guide from unsavoury incursions by the real; and luxury is nothing if not the relief from reality, an opiate that, far from delivering the 'experience' it promises, does all it can to stupefy the senses. But no need to beat yourself up: you've been working hard, you deserve a break. Why not put on the rose-tinted sunglasses for a week or two?

If such soft-focus imagery helps us ignore both the pressures of life at home and the realities pressing at the fringes of our resort – both where we were and where we are – it suggests that what we're buying when we book a trip is the chance to forget and that what the holiday packages is a pill. In which case, how does it square with that other motive behind booking a holiday, which is to have, if not always the 'experience of a lifetime', at least something to remember – not so trifling as a 'souvenir' (the very word means 'memory'), but maybe a memory with meaning? How does the holiday manage to join forgetting with remembering as seamlessly as sand and sea? Well, if, as thought by the Greeks, your mind resembles a house, then what the holiday does is exchange your domestic furniture for a set of foreign wares. For a blessed fortnight your familiar surroundings are packed up and shipped off, and once out of sight, they're out of mind; in their place a cargo of strange sensations and artefacts is unloaded. So, given that holidays are often dominated by sleep or a general relaxing of the mind, how is it that these foreign affairs ever get remembered? Because, by hosting a different set of images in your head – a change of scene within – you are doing exactly what's most likely to trigger the motor of your memory. For memory leans away from sameness towards difference; it harks after discontinuities, breaks, changes. Why else would you remember the twenty days of summer holiday you took as a child more vividly than the two hundred spent that year at school? The interruption of the holiday makes for greater image-brightness, and on just such dislocations memory thrives, growing not on the surface but in the cracks between the paving stones; when your life is boring, your memory stops paying attention, as if it were itself in a classroom sat in front of your life. So even as sea breezes shush you to sleep on a hammock, or you saunter along the sundown backstreets where grandmothers sit out on chairs, or you swallow another tumbler of the parish retsina, you are all the while populating your inner mansion with rich and strange portraits more likely, despite their transience, to linger after they've been deported.

In this net of forgetting-and-remembering that is the holiday's emblem, there's one thought that nearly always slips through – that the roots of the holiday reach not into luxury but austerity after all. As is obvious from the word, the holiday started as a 'holy day', a period given over to the self-denial appropriate beneath the unblinking gaze of God. And what makes self-denial appropriate? The regard for the body encouraged by luxury leads to a proportionate disregard for the soul, so better treat luxury as a threat to your moral health and abstain; if only in practical terms, the indulgent activities that luxury implies – the eating, the drinking, the being merry – will impair your concentration on higher things.

Older still than the holiday's heritage in austerity, however, is its provenance in the Lord's own recess, the sabbath. Because there's something virtuous about working, you'd guess there'd be something slothful about not, but no: there is a holiness in rest. Why? Only rest affords the time for contemplation, and contemplation has long been considered the royal road back to the Almighty, the one who instituted that first break. It's hard to give God his due when you're taken up with daily life. And because the holiday, this sabbath of the soul, is both a time for reflecting on God and a reprise of his own sabbatical, it counts, in the words of Coleridge, as a repetition, in the finite life of the individual, of the infinite life of the deity. In short, the holiday is sublime.

The trouble is that once you vacate work, the day hollowed out for holiness assumes the vacant form of a vacation, and that leaves it open not just to sacred observances but to pleasurable distractions – the path to the Almighty is a narrow one, with virtue down one side and, down the other, vice. It's an ambivalence exhibited in the word 'vacation' itself, which, far more neutral than 'holiday' (it practically *means* neutrality), refuses to dictate how to use the time off; so that whereas a holiday relieves you from work but refers to at least the vestiges of religious obligation, a vacation proclaims open season.

Those two poles of penance and pleasure entwined long ago, as it happens, to form the practice of pilgrimage. Taking asceticism to a new level, the pilgrimage would enact what St John of the Cross, a Spanish mystic of the sixteenth century, named the 'dark night of the soul', a boldly going through the psyche's most blighted reaches, a wading into the deathly valleys that corrugate the heart, to reach a place of revealed truth. This internal drama takes external form as a reconstruction of the Stations of the Cross, whereby Christ, dead man walking, hefted his own instrument of torture through the streets to be splayed upon it. This hysterical scene in the Christian tradition has parallels, of course – in Islam as the frenzied convergence upon Mecca, in Judaism as the zealous falling-fever at Jerusalem's Wailing Wall – and while all that passionate intensity adds to the pilgrim's stock in heaven, it can't quite prevent the pilgrimage from being a bit of an adventure on earth. Its end couldn't be more solemn, but the means of the pilgrimage being a journey, a foray into the unfamiliar, makes for a mischievous confusion. Hardly surprising, really: you're away from work, away from home, and bound en route to meet with all sorts of worldly distractions, nay temptations. It was just such inevitable deviation from the straight and narrow path that animated Chaucer to write his own pilgrimage pastiche, the *Canterbury Tales*, a comic tract on how what goes up must come down, how High Church meets low life, how the Vulgate (the then standard translation of the Bible from Greek to Latin) becomes vulgar. The motley crew of pilgrims that gathers for the horse ride from London to Kent, to worship at the bones of Thomas Becket, can't help having fun along the way. Centuries before mass tourism took off in the twentieth, the pilgrimage had amply staged the adulteration of the sacred by the profane that continues to cloud the choices you make today, as you book your getaway, dithering as to which to put first – what feels good or what feels right.

Susceptible though the pilgrimage is to such ambiguities in its set-up, its end – now not the spiritual, but the geographical terminus – remains clear, and if each year thousands flock to Canterbury or Santiago de Compostela, it's for a reason: the place is special. Even if pilgrimages think of places as platforms for communing with the divine, their fixation with them still makes the physical location special in itself, and this is what they have bequeathed the holiday most. As Walter Benjamin – our flâneur from the previous chapter – points out, the more something can be replicated, the more its aura fades, a maxim from which the place can only benefit. For a place is *what* it is mainly by virtue of *where* it is, and so by definition it can't be replicated – if you reproduce it elsewhere, it's no longer placed where it was, no longer the place it was – which makes it more likely than any other kind of thing to accrue an aura of its own. So all places have it, this aura, but it would be false to deny that some have more than others – compared to its suburbs, the cathedral in Krakow, say, has something special. The example might sound random, but extra-special places are all members of a more-or-less recognised canon that might include Adam's Peak, where the first man first set foot on earth; Mount Ararat, where Noah's Ark got pinioned after the Flood; the wise assembly of monoliths at Stonehenge; or the slow-release potency of Angkor Wat. More than irreplaceable, these places seem to have a genius loci, a spirit of the place, over and above their topographic singularity. But isn't that because, you might ask, they're all sacred? No doubt. Even so, a place can now gain membership of this club without having been sanctified, thanks to the brilliance with which the holiday took up its bequest, a brilliance that lies in identifying sub-sacred destinations and conferring on them an extra-special status, an aura, willy-nilly. Perhaps to the naked eye, Everest has become a tawdry rat-run for jocks, Copenhagen's Little Mermaid an underdressed lifebuoy, the steps at Odessa a tedious cut-through to the beach, but all of them radiate, all have achieved that mysterious pull.

Apart from sacredness, then, in what does this aura consist? What is it about the holiday destination that gets the saliva glands pulsing? To define it is to deplete it, but three ingredients are vital. First and foremost, the holiday destination is the anticipated realisation of a thought – when we visit it, the place *comes true*, and there's a magic in that. Second, having invested money and effort in the journey there, we're going to make sure we get a return, so what steams off the monument that we've paid to marvel at is partly our own projection on to it. Third, the holiday destination becomes special because people keep going to it because other people said it was special who went there because other people said it was special, and so on ad infinitum. Then, as if that weren't enough, there's the negative power acquired by such destinations – that is, seeing them is great, but *not* seeing them produces a deficit in your life experience, a pleasure to be expiated almost like a pain. These are places that are not just 'nice to see' but a 'must see', a visit without which life itself supposedly will be poorer and less lived – *Vedere Napoli e poi morire*: see Naples and then die.

You have only to think of the Las Vegas effect, however, to give that argument a sharp correction. For if Las Vegas proves anything, it's that places are as replicable as anything else, their auras kidnapped as fleetly as souls. Much as in the film sets of the state next door, the Nevadan neopolis has remade 'Venice' and 'New York' in their own image, erecting almost full-scale replicas; and even improved on them, in so far as only the best bits have been kept, with any unpleasant-nesses deodorised. In this respect, they become what Jean Baudrillard, the French postmodernist, called a 'simulacrum', a supposed copy that effectively becomes more original than the original, and so plays havoc with our sense of what's real and what's not (and one might think of places like Magaluf in Majorca, colonised by British tourists to such an extent that it is more British than anything back home). One consequence must be that seeing Venice after seeing 'Venice' will be a disappointment, the copy having asset-stripped the original and overtaken it, a consequence you might want to resist. You might, for instance, be thinking that if such is postmodernism, you'd prefer to dismiss it as an unfortunate new development – and yet this artificial process of recreation, of which Vegas marks a climax, is not so modern, after all. It began much earlier, from the first moment, in fact, that places started to appear in reproductions. Yes, Las Vegas might have done it in 3D, but 2D versions of destinations circulated hundreds, if not thousands, of years before. The most famous example must be the etchings of Rome by Piranesi, which inspired the Grand Tour generation to sign up for the trip to the cradle of civilisation. So impressive were Piranesi's visual, almost gothic, accounts of the Colosseum, the Tomb of Caecilia Metella and the ruins of the Forum that the grand tourists couldn't fail, upon arrival, to feel let down. Perhaps they should have stayed at home.

But perhaps you can be on holiday even when you are at home. I'm not referring to the fad for the 'staycation', but to the phenomenon, as developed by Jacques Derrida, himself a famously globetrotting academic, of being permanently on leave – by remaining away from yourself. It's a theme elaborated in a book called *The Post Card*, a series of imaginary postcards on philosophical themes. In it, Derrida argues that our sense of being comes from sending ourselves messages, as manifested in literally hearing ourselves speak. The trouble is that the messages are subject to getting corrupted. Or, being no different from the message you might send someone on a postcard, the message you send yourself can always be lost or stolen in transit. Why is that? Well, if messages weren't susceptible to getting hijacked, you wouldn't be able to send them at all – otherwise, how would they ever be free to detach themselves from you and go on their way? The only sure means of guaranteeing that your message arrives is to hold on to it throughout: but if you never let go, it can never be received. So before it returns to you, an interval has to fall during which the self-addressed message might be purloined or simply vanish, effectively a gap between you and yourself. Even when the message returns home safely, it will have been exposed to this difference that shoots like a crack down your very being. In short, you're always on holiday from yourself, consigned to writing yourself postcards that may or may not be delivered.

And if, even sitting in your armchair at home, you therefore inhabit dual time zones, it raises the question of time travel itself – probably the ultimate holiday. This isn't to say we won't keep pushing the limits of travelling in space – and literally so, as tickets for space travel went on sale some while ago – but that the Holy Grail of holiday destinations lies not in the wider galaxy but in time. Of course, we already possess, in the faculty of memory, the gift of time travel, whereby the merest waft of a certain perfume can take us back to a specific date in our youth – in which we follow Proust who, in his compendious *Remembrance of Things Past*, derived a million words of recollection from a single taste of madeleine. But to physically travel through time remains the final frontier. Is that what you should be saving up for?

Perhaps. But for all the wonder associated with it, time travel may not be so different from a regular holiday. When you travel through time you're never an innocent bystander; there's always the chance you might disturb the past or future in a way analogous with how, as a holidaymaker, you create an effect, however small, in the destination you've arrived at. You might not agree with those cultural theorists who construe tourism as a latter-day form of colonial mastery, a devious expression of empire, but you might accept that your presence abroad has some kind of impact. From your first exchange with the taxi driver at the airport to what you leave in the hotel bathroom for the chambermaid, you are sending small percussions through the local system. And yet, because we all need a break, we're never not going to book our holidays, so the trick is to reverse the perspective. If you want to be a good visitor, and not feel guilty about exploiting the natives, or using up all that aviation fuel, the thing is to be a good host – when tourists arrive from around the world in your own home-land, treat them well. If what you look for when booking a holiday is, in part, great hospitality from your host, the best you can do is return the favour.

Either way, the point is that you are never 'away' at all – wherever you are, you're always there. And if you're always there, it might be that holidays are less of an escape than those brochures lead us to believe. If you're trying to 'get away from it all', it might be worth pondering what it is you're trying to get away from. If it's home that you want to leave, then instead of putting so much thought into your holiday, which lasts for only a fraction of the year, that effort might be better invested in making your home ideal. Equally, if you go on holiday to 'find yourself', it might be simpler – and cheaper – to find yourself in your own backyard. It's a sentiment implicit in the words of Ralph Waldo Emerson: 'Though we travel the world over to find the beautiful, we must carry it with us or we find it not.'

10

Going to the gym

WHEN IN LA, do as the Angelinos do: drive to the gym. It's obvious that if you didn't drive but walked – or, better still, jogged – you might not need the fitness club you had arrived at, saving time, petrol and membership fees in the process; but not obvious – or persuasive – enough to deter thousands of Californians from doing exactly that. Because these citizens go nowhere without the automobile, they're forced to compensate for so sedate an existence by making a special effort to get the heart rate above sixty beats per minute. The car that chauffeurs its passengers to the gym thus has the complex function of helping to spare them from the physical inertia to which it has damned them.

Along with office work, Internet shopping and TV, cars conspire to keep modern life on its *derrière* and the gym has been evolved, like an iron lung, to supply the resulting want of exercise. But it doesn't follow that the gym is the only answer. Even if a jog around the neighbourhood makes you self-conscious, doing crunches on your bedroom carpet feels absurd, or rhythmically clenching your buttocks at your desk invites suspicion, there are, apart from those individual pursuits, plenty of team games, like football or volleyball, which enjoy an altogether less eccentric profile and permit a throbbing of the heart, a blooming of the cheek, that's perfectly acceptable in polite society. Aerobic alternatives abound, but all around the world gyms keep opening up. Why?

Self-management, in part. For one thing, team games take some organising, whereas gym-going is a unilateral affair, within your control, a module in a week that you will customise with other modules like seeing friends, taking in a movie or doing your shopping. And if team games need organising, it's because teams need people, and if teams need people, people need space, space generally means going outside and outside has weather. At its simplest, the gym offers all the advantages of sport without the disadvantage of rain, wind or too fierce a sun. Even if the phrase 'indoor sports' harbours a contradiction – really, exercise should go with fresh air and connect us back to when, as a species, exercise wasn't an optional extra – this all-weather benefit is key because, by removing the meteorological hazard, it acknowledges that desire for personal control and enables it. In so doing, the gym reverses man and nature: when you pelt across fields, nature is larger than you; when you scamper on a treadmill, it gets shrunk to a slot in your diary. The magnitude of life has been managed into a moment of lifestyle and that is not all bad. This isn't to say other benefits – like jogging without having to dodge pedestrians or litter – don't factor, but taken together, those two requirements – that you can do it alone and in all weathers – mean going to the gym can be fitted in with your lifestyle needs, and, in a world that barges you about, that is a prize not to be sniffed at.

The individualism in the gym proposition is endorsed by the experience itself. Though an ostensibly democratic space, rarely so 'exclusive' that it will turn custom away, the gym presents a sheltered environment, designed to produce in its visitors more inwardness than outwardness; despite your body being on display, and your having to heave and sweat – both externalising forces – the mood proper to the gym is more introvert than extrovert. For in combining exertion with concentration and, in the locker room, ablution with being on display, a certain bracing of the self is called for, a girding of one's boundaries very different from the indolence possible while mooching about a flea market, or riffling through *Vogue*: having been made so aware of your edges, you're more inclined to guard them – it's still significant that the word 'gymnasium' comes from the Greek for 'naked'. The effect is of privacy in public, a sheathing of the self, which makes the gym less a forum for breezy civic congregation than a hive of composite privacies – whose symbol might be the headphones that insulate against the gurning, expectorating and muscular strife all about.

In this respect, the rules of the gym resemble those in places of worship. While a synagogue – a word that means 'coming together' – and a church – where the word 'ecclesiastic', like *'église'* in French, means 'a calling together' – summon the faithful to muster, that convergent energy soon diverges, as if through an hourglass, into the separating practice of prayer, where each person becomes a grain of sand again, and the private conversation with God may begin. In the gym, prayer mats metamorphose into floor mats, and prayer cushions steps, but the hourglass movement persists: even if you've come for a class – body sculpting, Pilates, spinning, circuits – rather than the stoic challenge of racking yourself singly to rowing machine or bench press, the group activity soon gives way to an unmediated negotiation with yourself and yourself alone. And although that sounds forbidding, it might, like a call from your conscience, feel undeniable. For on the map of the mind, it is at the X of conscience that exercise and prayer gather, both recalling you to a duty, and a duty, moreover, that can be discharged by no one else. Perhaps that's what conscience is – the sense of a debt that can't be signed over, and so an intimation of one's own essential solitude. Only you can make that investment but, equally, only you can take the return.

However, the main reason for the individuation enjoined on us by the gym is to do not with its spiritual but with its physical demands, and in this the gym resembles less the church than the hospital. Already connected on the spectrum from prevention to cure, gym and hospital both hold up a mirror to your body – and force a confrontation with it. The fact that where the gym visit is discretionary the hospital appointment firmly isn't, makes no odds: once inside, your body stands on trial, and as they envy or sympathise with the physical hand you've been dealt, everyone around you knows it; with degrees of slyness, all gym-goers, like all inpatients, wonder about the vitality or otherwise of the bodies trooping past. Less discretionary still and, in its refusal to be transferred, similar to that debt of conscience is the impossibility of being dealt a different hand – that is, swapping your body, or becoming separated from it, for the merest nanosecond. Even more than your mind, which can be stolen by indoctrination, your body can never be divorced from you and who you are – odd, considering the mind is where we think the self is principally located. No matter how close you might get to someone else – in combat, say, or coitus – this own-ness of your body can never be decreased, and it's something we experience with particular intensity at the gym. You may well cruise up to the gym in a car – the device supreme for relieving its passengers of their bodyfulness, for minimising human effort – but that car won't ever unseat your body from you. More importantly, your body is that without which your exercise routine can't commence, which is the key link to the hospital. Like undergoing surgery, working out can't be done on your behalf, so that where most other tasks – from fetching the milk to firing a mortar – may be delegated, this one, this work of getting the pulse pumping, insists that you are the only man or woman for the job. If we could pay the personal trainer to exercise for us, we probably would, but we can only delegate so much, limited to outsourcing the willpower needed to make our workout happen. As for the rest – the plucky encounter with our undismissable bodies – it is up to us. The gym projects into your diary an intimate date with your embodied, living self.

Ultimately, of course, the reason for going to either gym or hospital is to stave off death, or at least to defer it as long as possible. Here it's worth thinking about Martin Heidegger, the twentieth century's most formidable German philosopher, who, pondering the fact of mortality from his shack in the Black Forest, argued that your very being is granted only on the condition that it will one day come to an end – not least, of course, because your body will give out. That makes the body you take to the gym a peculiar alloy of two things – both the vehicle of your living, as well as the reason why you'll die. After all, if you didn't have a body, you wouldn't be susceptible to death, and you'd have no reason for going to the gym in the first place. What you see at the gym is bodies attempting to resist the fact that they are bodies – that is, natural entities bound one day to give up the ghost. That you do have a body means on the treadmill, you are running for your life.

Fortunately, there's something about running that brings the liveness that you do have especially alive and seems to put death behind you. London has a store selling trainers called Run and Become, a name that gets to the heart of the energetic connection between running and existence. Of course, you can stand there and just be, you can lie on a couch munching doughnuts and just be, but for your being to become itself, to burst into a flame of beingness, there's nothing quite like running. That's partly because running feels primal, even feral – as we run we become an animal in the human race – it asks you to summon your aliveness and make everything kinetic, transfuse all white into red, as if there were no greater effort. And in this, running expresses one of life's essential properties, which is the capacity to run by itself: to pick itself up by its own bootstraps, to displace itself without external force acting upon it. Being has this godlike power to mobilise itself, to motor itself, to be auto-motive – your body is an *automobile* that, unlike the duplicitous car, needs no ignition to get it going.

Compared to that Volkswagen you drove to the gym, then, you are a superior entity. That is the good news. The bad news is that this body that moves by itself may not be so uniquely yours, after all. A moment ago, I was describing the immutable, isotopic relationship between your body and you, the complete identity of the two. But go into any weights room in any gym and you will see its occupants quite unconcernedly reshaping their bodies, chipping contours from the blob they began as, retrieving form from formlessness. True, the weights room attracts a particular type, so the sample may be off, but the fact that anyone, after a few stints with the dumb-bells, can define their deltoids, transform their trapezoids and puff the biceps into hillocks on the arm means that, only so many reps away, a different body awaits. That different body might still be your 'ownmost', to use a Heidegger word – something utterly inalienable – but what's the value of ownmostness if it applies to things so easily refashioned? It seems cheap. What's more, because such bodily improvements tend to be undertaken in view of an ideal, they generate a physique not more but less unique: the gain in perfection comes with some loss of character, with some smoothing out, as for a Barbie Doll, of the dehiscences, declivities and dewlaps that are exclusively yours.

But perhaps that's a wilful misunderstanding. Heidegger, for one, would say that remoulding your body is a far cry from transforming your being – getting buff might conceivably alter *who* you are, but it won't change *that* you are. Regardless of the strength gained on the resistance machines by your *pectoralis major*, when it comes to resisting the ultimate force – death – muscle failure must set in; OK, with each yank on the pulley, you shunt death backwards a few minutes more, but you'll never disarm it of its secret weapon – the fact that it's inevitable. Death may be a question of when, but never a question of whether.

A forceful argument in itself, to be sure, and yet the iron weight of Heidegger's reason can be pushed against too, and since his own inevitable passing, much of European philosophy has involved the dismantling of what in Heidegger is, like a discarded cycling machine, the rusting framework of old-school philosophy. Although Heidegger himself railed against what philosophy had become – so many technical distinctions that make no difference – in order to call philosophy back to its original purpose, of understanding the nature of being, the truth is that 'being' itself represents the final bastion of the philosophical establishment, the last stand of metaphysics – and the gym heralds the next generation. For the gym supports the lifestyle values that fly in the face of oh-so-philosophical 'life', with its burden of being and its debt to death – as if the physical took a look at the metaphysical and saw it could outrun it. You're not exactly in denial about death when you go to the gym, but health and fitness belong squarely in this world, the world of the visible and manageable; even if it does reach right into your heart to wind it up, the gym is more about the superficial benefits, the glowing skin, the firmer stomach, the shape-lier legs. Such goals may have their sights set short of The End itself, but they constitute ends in themselves – and in this they are well served by the phrase 'working out': it doesn't say you're working out a problem, or working out your notice – no, you're simply working out, a self-directed agent set in a hazy cocoon of physical activity. No need to bother with all those obscure throwbacks like 'being', which can be proved no more than God; just run on past them as if they were the last burning patch of oil from the Dark Ages, soon to be extinguished.

So the gym helps usurp life with lifestyle, to depose that scholastic and unyielding state of 'being' for the sake of new – and renewable – identity. Which sounds like a good thing, a revolution which puts power, like a barbell, back in our hands – unless we're all deluded. I said a moment ago that the gym tends in the opposite direction, to reduce the differences between bodies and favour identikit over iden-tity, but there are people who go further. We're familiar, for instance, with 'body fascism', the notion that, if you want to belong, your body must conform to a certain type – not too fat, not too short, not too wrinkly. It's a set of rules that disadvantages women in particular, where fat is a feminist issue because it pronounces against curves, demanding that the natural female excrescences of breasts, bottoms and hips be kept under control. But it also applies to gay men, where a different type – cropped hair, narrow waist, sinewy shoulders – seems just as mandatory. Far from representing a treasured island of indi-vidual self-creation, the gym can be seen as a colony of bondage, a cult of sameness or a ministry of size that grades bodies according to whether they are aesthetically, and therefore socially, passable. And because this emphasis on the body goes with a de-emphasis on the mind, it's as if a tacit suppression, rather than promotion, of genuine individuality, of different voices, were at work. Perhaps it's expressed in the actual silence of exercise – gyms are notable for the contrast between the ambient noise of TVs, tannoys and whirring treadmills, and its denizens' voiceless striving – which suggests you're focusing too much on your body to worry about who you are.

The argument can be taken further still. This stifling of the individual might mean the gym has become the parade ground of what Michel Foucault names 'docile bodies', humans unwittingly subjected to the needs of the state, docile rather than dissenting, bodies rather than minds. Instead of facilitating our personal schedule, the gym has a schema of its own that we are fitted into: it views us as units to be organised around a timetable that's scarcely different from the roster in a factory or a house of correction. True, your labour in the gym has no output from which the state might benefit – except in so far as your increased health means a decreased strain on welfare – but as a building where your comings and goings are logged, your medical data stored, your deviation from the norm measured, the gym has become a state institution, a real-time census of what the proles are up to – though, as we'll see in a moment, there are ways of getting your own back.

And if Foucault's approach sounds somewhat paranoid, you need only think of the authority that gyms have acquired by laying hold of the formerly amateur affair of keeping fit and professionalising it. We've long passed the time when it was possible, without feeling like a chump, to do star jumps on the patio, for example, because exercise has been handed over, via the gym, to science, and back again. Today it's not merely amateur to exercise outside the strip-lit and increasingly clinical rooms of the gym, it's positively dangerous, and the smooth-skinned graduates in sports science who patrol the gym carry monitors that bleep the subliminal message of 'Don't try this at home'; look around at the gym's special furniture – the computerised cardio machines, the fitness regime memory cards, the prints of human anatomy – and that message is only amplified. The gym is out to convince you that you can't be trusted with your own body, so it's better left to the experts; and if conscience is the first lever that pulls you back to the gym, this subtle admonition as to your incompetence is the second.

So let's say Foucault is right – the gym is a wolf in sheep's clothing, an overtly friendly club on a covert mission to monitor not just your heart rate but your general regularity as a subject. And now turn that argument on its head. The state wouldn't need to keep bodies docile if they didn't hold the power to subvert it, which is to reconceive the body as a political weapon, an agent of resistance. It's an idea developed by Foucault's precursor, Mikhail Bakhtin, who grew up amid the Russian Revolution and argued for the body's dissident force, its ability to escape from the norms prescribed on high. For, like a garden, the body is naturally wild, prone to disorder, and the less hedged about it is, the more it symbolises the power of the people to overgrow their institutional fences.

To Bakhtin, the body was a 'carnival' (the very word refers to 'flesh'), a festival with the power to turn the world upside down and license the licentiousness of physical abandon; and if the body was susceptible to knock knees, a humped back or cellulite, so much the better, for this tendency to exceed its own boundaries was a literal embodiment of the body politic as it should be – plural, populist and given to performance. To the hypothesis that the gym is a state-run enterprise that takes in irregular raw material, in order to transform it into regular shapes, the answer should therefore be to ransack and replace it with the anti-gym – a gallery of misfits not unlike a painting by Hieronymus Bosch or a sculpture by the Chapman Brothers, where bodies come in all shapes and sizes, deformity is welcome and obesity a sign of self-expression. Assuming your own body falls somewhat short of Venus or Adonis, you needn't, therefore, despair – each surplus inch around the waist speaks to the revolutionary in you.

11

Taking a bath

ON WIKIHOW – the more vocational, less academic cousin of Wikipedia – you will find the following instructions for taking a bath:

1. Take off your clothes and put them in a pile neatly. Then prepare your tub. **Make sure you close the door!**
2. **Find a water-holding enclosure big enough for you to fit in.** The obvious choice would be a bathtub, but anything big enough and deep enough will work. Be sure that it is water-tight to avoid leaking (and to keep anything else from getting in). You could use a hole dug in the ground with some form of sealant, or a natural water-holding formation such as a basin within stone.
3. **Fill the tub with water.** If you have a bathtub built into your shelter of choice, you probably have running water available. If so, turn the faucet on. If not, try using buckets to bring water from your water source to your tub. Fill it until there is enough water to submerge your body in. Keep in mind that the water level will rise by way of displacement when you get in.
4. **Choose your water temperature.** Cold baths have their appeal for some, but most prefer to relax with a hot bath. If you have a water heater, odds are that the water came out of the faucet at the temperature you want. If you don't, you can still heat your water. One way would be to build a fire next to your bath, but you risk

their own right, a display of industrial prowess). Either way, and with their walk-in access, their slate tiles and the botanical extractions for lathering the locks of its occupants, the modern shower aims to be a thermal grotto, a hot spring that gurgles magically from your wall as if from a limestone cave, suppressing its technical elements and so copying the easiness of the bath. But the technical always threatens to tip into the clinical, and the feeling of being steamed in soothing vapours soon becomes vulnerability. This is especially true of the shower enclosed by Perspex doors that, while trying to create a safety capsule for your privacy and comfort, turn it into a transponder or scanning device from which you could emerge with your protons rearranged. And although you are standing up, making for an alertness you'll struggle to achieve in the bath, your nakedness is all the more exposed than in the engulfing tub. Opt for a shower curtain, if you like, but, as we were reminded by Alfred Hitchcock – who did for bathrooms what Spielberg did for beaches – it can't guarantee as much protection as it might.

This isn't to say that the bath doesn't have hair-raising features of its own. Its coffin shape evokes the corpse stiffening within it, the association with 'acid bath' reminds one of the notorious John George Haigh's victims and the threat of an electric current being passed through its deceptively placid lake is only a hairdryer away. Then, in other clinics, you have the still less glamorous 'sponge bath' – that pathetic supine sopping and mopping of the frail and infirm. Yet all of those are somehow comic and forgivable: to the tragic scaffold of the shower, the bath is a Vaudeville prop, a pint-size reservoir for toy boats, where bath is short for bathos. Perhaps this levelling that the bath produces has to do not just with its horizontal aspect but with the disabling effect of being in water, the resistance to its motion that renders the body feeble or inept, as if hampered like astronauts. By slowing us down, the bath humanises us – it acknowledges the humanness of the human species, as beings who rest as well as work, who have a need, no matter how grown up, and how far they've aged since they were babies bathed at bathtime, to be cradled in its uterine waters. Baby showers, yes, but showering babies, no – the bath is the place for this everyday return to our beginning.

So much so that, as amnesiac as it is amniotic, the bath will even lull you to sleep (an impossibility in the shower). But if sleep brings the risk of drowning, then you can stop short of snoozing with meditation. These days the bath, in the West, likes to pretend it's in the East, appointing itself with candles, oils and subdued lighting that together evoke a watery shrine, a lotus pool for floatation and fathomless relaxation. However, contrary to popular belief, the meditative state encouraged by Buddhism, at least, aims for relaxation's reverse – not the easeful drifting of your thoughts, but heightened consciousness. And 'heightened consciousness' is not the same as a high, a seeing the world as if on acid; nor the superabundant sense of yourself spilling over with brilliance; nor yet the acquisition of superpowers, as if you were an action hero capable of listening in to the crackling of life on Mars. In the Buddhist tradition, heightened consciousness – the aim of meditation – means living completely in the moment, such that you become intensely aware of everything around you, right down to the difference in temperature felt at the entrance to your nostrils, between the air that you breathe in – try it – and that you breathe out. And what's so great about that? By practising this meditative *'bhavana'* (to use the Sanskrit word), you train your mind not to wander, and thereby spare yourself unnecessary suffering. For almost irresistibly, your thoughts as you lie there soaking will turn into fantasies – the person you'd like to kiss, the pay rise you've been anticipating – and fantasies put you into a state of wanting, of reaching for something beyond the moment. Which is bad because, according to the Buddha, wanting is what suffering springs from. It creates an attachment to things, by which you become enslaved; like foam bubbles twinkling on a tepid bath, wanting provides superficial interest, some pearlescent wonder to divert you, while what lies beneath – your ability to live in the present – is going cold. By drawing you back to the here and now, meditation weakens the addictive fascination with objects of fantasy. In or out of the bath, it has the twin advantage of calming the craving that corrodes you and enabling you to tune in to the plain wonder of what is.

It was something like this higher consciousness that led to one of the greatest discoveries of all time, and one which took place during the most celebrated bathtime ever. This, of course, was the original eureka moment when Greek philosopher-scientist Archimedes discovered the law of displacement. Unable to consult wikiHow, he had to use his own scientific ingenuity to solve the problem he'd been set, of whether the king's crown was really made of solid gold or had been mixed with cheaper metal that allowed its maker to make more of a profit – and without harming the crown by chipping away at it or melting it down. Sitting in his suds, Archimedes realised he could ascertain whether the crown had the density of pure gold by dropping it in and seeing if it displaced as much water as it should, that is, whether the density matched the volume. 'Eureka!' he said, and went off dancing down the road, in the sheer delight at having discovered this new law of physics.

As well as the genius of the discovery itself, the anecdote reveals a number of things about taking a bath. Set aside the obvious point that here was a philosopher doing something we wouldn't naturally associate with men of the mind (it's said that Jean-Paul Sartre never bathed in case it took time away from the higher things in life, such as thinking, talking, smoking and having sex with the impressively tolerant Simone de Beauvoir). The eureka moment reveals the bath's capacity, like a bain-marie, to unfreeze the mind and allow the creative juices to flow, to transmute it from torpor to meditative brightness to puncturing insight (perhaps every lab should have one, just as media agencies have sofas), even if the breakthrough is qualified by the again comic connotations of the bath, and the less than dignified caper through town. Capacity is the thing: Archimedes lit on displacement as a physical law, but there's a metaphysical axis too. When you get into your bath and see the levels rise in precise proportion to your own volume, the water gives you a more palpable reading than the air ever could of the fact that your cubic capacity takes up space, and space, moreover, that can't be occupied at the same time by anything else. The world moves around you always, hugging you close as water, but by the same token allows your viscous slipping through it. OK, your bodily system isn't quite so sealed as that suggests – apart from the orifices that give out or take in matter, the bath itself will turn your fingers wrinkly as they absorb more of it – but for the most part, you cleave the elements you move in like a seal, and the bath reconfirms the fact that your being is an integrated mass of atoms whose very integrity is what makes you what you are.

What you are, at least, so long as that integrity withstands disintegration, the eventual atomisation of your body and its return to the elements. Worse things happen at sea, of course, and yet if we *were* to dissolve in the bath, there wouldn't be much evidence to prove it. The statistics vary, but as biology teachers like to insist, at least 70 per cent of your body is water, so all that would be left would be a few teeth floating and, in a tragicomic swansong, a rubber duck slaloming among them. This affinity between humans and water – which dates from the archaic period when proto-humans were unicellular organisms bobbing in the biotic soup of the primordial oceans – has even had an impact on the theory of evolution. For if getting into the bath feels so natural, it might be for prehistoric reasons. The accepted wisdom says that apes began evolving into men at the point where they shimmied down from the trees of the jungle and started trekking, upright, across the savannah. But there's an alternative theory that goes back to Archimedes's own intellectual ancestor, Anaximander, and it argues that, before developing on dry land, the early hominid must have been a swimmer. Known today as the theory of the 'aquatic ape', and associated most with the multi-talented Welsh writer Elaine Morgan, it posed the following questions, with the implicit answer that 'man' – and indeed 'woman' – was being equipped to swim with the fishes:

+ Why, if not to enable them to move better through water, do humans, unlike other mammals, not have bodily hair to speak of?
+ Why, like dolphins, do they have a layer of subcutaneous fat?

+ Why, if not for better lubrication, do they (again unlike other mammals) have sebaceous glands in their skin?

The 'aquatic ape' theory may have its detractors, but it doesn't mean we have to throw the baby out with the bathwater. Whether or not it provides the missing link in the narrative of the rise of man, it reinforces the fact that, for a mammal, *Homo sapiens* is remarkably adept in water, a born Aquarian who's at home in the bath for reasons that are more than psychological.

The connection goes deeper still. Not only are we made of water and swim happily in its liquid lap, there may even be a kind of 'morphic resonance', to use the phrase of cutting-edge physicist Rupert Sheldrake, between us and H_2O (we also need water to survive, let us not forget, and so vital is it that the Latin word *'aqua'* is an abbreviation of a phrase that's something like 'what we need to draw from in order to live'). In 1999, on the islands of Japan, Masaru Emoto published extraordinary research making the case that 'water is a mirror reflecting our mind'. His book *The Message from Water* is an album of photographs of water crystals from around the world and in different states. Emoto wouldn't actually need any of the astonishing claims he goes on to make for the crystals themselves to astonish us: they are as beautiful as diamond jewellery, and with a similarly uncanny effect of nature combined with artifice. But the mainly beautiful, princess-like crystals have some ugly sisters. While the water crystals photographed at Japan's Metori Yusui spring are like angel candy, the spitting image of celestial radiance, those at Sapporo, a city of two million people, while 'trying desperately to be clean', are malformed, even mutant – not that all cities are bad for their crystals, and Buenos Aires, for example, is honoured with crystals like exquisite medallions. There's already an implication that water responds to how it's treated by human beings, and it's only made more explicit when Emoto's research team explores the effect on the crystals of playing them music. Bach elicits predictably heavenly formations; heavy metal forces a concentric explosion in the crystalline form; and, most captivatingly of all, Chopin's 'Farewell

Song' causes the elements of the crystal to separate from one another, as if in departure. The team then 'shows' phrases to the water, by which an already spooky experiment becomes spookier still. They divide a sample of distilled water between two bottles:

> We then pasted a paper on one bottle that had 'Thank you' typed on it. On the other bottle we put 'You fool'. We then left them both that way for the night. The next day we froze this water and took pictures of the crystals that formed.

Guess what? The water that has been thanked rewards the researchers with perfect crystals, while the other batch produces disfigured shapes. From Roman baths to hotel spas, taking the waters has often been thought of as benefiting our health – we even think the lowly domestic bathtub can help a bit, a hot bath nearly always a good thing – but that we might affect the health of the water is quite a finding. It suggests we are part of a unified field and that when you're in your bath, you are literally in your element – or rather your body and your own muddying waters are pretty much the same, part of a sympathetic system, with messages flowing both ways.

Perhaps this is another way of accounting for water's intrinsic neutrality. Although its mineral content will vary, and its purity depend on this or that (Los Angeles has a bar serving as many varietals of water as wine), water is always the same nothing. This isn't to say it isn't everything – it constitutes about the same proportion of the earth's surface as it does our bodies – but that water surpasses even the colour white in its basal ability to be the medium of everything else, the über-host of the world, and indeed the very thing that Mars would need to start a family of living creatures. So as you marinate yourself next time in your suds, you might enjoy not just the solace that it brings – assuming, of course, that you've followed wikiHow to the letter – but also the fact that you are reconnecting with the vital ingredient of being, the source that made both you and all your ancestors possible.

12

Reading a book

DEAR READER, by the end of this sentence you will have read the first one of this chapter, but won't be any the wiser. This second sentence hardly helps, because it too discusses only itself. As for the third, well, it follows the first and second in its refusal to point to anything in the outside world.

The paragraph you've just read is grammatically correct, but irritatingly meaningless. As a piece of language, it might constitute a technically good use, but it is also an abuse, for language should refer to something real, with words standing in for things. At least, that is the classic conception of language as voiced, for example, by St Augustine in his *Confessions*, and glossed, in his *Philosophical Investigations*, by the Cambridge whiz-kid Ludwig Wittgenstein, as the idea that 'every word has a meaning'.

If only it were that simple.

What really happens when you read a sentence like this, let alone a whole book? For a book is made up of words, and words are remarkable things. How is it that black squiggles printed on paper are capable of streaming like tiny bats off the page and into your mind, where they create a silent pandemonium to upset you, amuse you, move you, frighten you or even turn you on? The classical theory itself was split between two schools of thought, both described by Plato. The first, spoken through the personage of Cratylus, says it's because words truly are connected to real things and that the connecting tissue is organic, a continuous tendon that binds them to each other. Take the word 'sea', for example: it would have to enjoy a natural link to the heaving bulk of saltwater that pools around the contours of the planet's land masses, and so much so that the brine itself demands being spoken of with a word of one syllable and three letters, beginning with 's' and ending with 'a'. Word derives from thing as congenitally as child descends from parent.

Except that 'sea' is an English term, not the *'thalassa'* that Plato knew, so what makes it a more natural word for the waters of the ocean than the Greek or, for that matter, the Arabic *'al bahr'* or the French *'la mer'*, or indeed any other of the hundreds of terms for the sea that exist among the myriad languages spoken around the globe? The ancient Cratylus might have envisaged a natural connection between words and things, but from our travels we moderns know that people use wildly different words to denote the same item, and when our hire car breaks down on holiday, things go much more smoothly if we know the translation for 'carburettor'. Hence the rival school of thought: the relationship between words and things is not natural, but artificial. As long as we all agreed to be bound by it, it wouldn't matter a jot if we substituted the word 'sea' for something else – even something completely made up, like 'cudmoil', 'phenactic' or 'blorus' – and in any case, these days we're much more comfortable with neologisms: podcasting, obamania, blogosphere … we've embraced them all.

And if words are a matter of convention, you could go further, as did Wittgenstein himself, and argue that conventions are only made up in particular moments. When a builder shouts to a carpenter to toss him the screwdriver, he cares little for its abstract definition – he's not requesting that the carpenter pass him 'a tool for turning screws', but is picturing the Phillips with the red handle in the carpenter's belt, and when he starts to tighten the screw, the torsion becomes part of the screwdriver's meaning, as does the wardrobe he's assembling, and the client who's watching over his shoulder; together they create a miniature but meaningful event like a playlet or what Wittgenstein called a 'language-game'. The game works on a set of local rules invented and played out as necessary.

It may not be hard to reject Cratylus, or even accept Wittgenstein, but the consequences of doing so are more startling than you might think. For, as randomly chosen sounds and signs, as mere markers for things in the world, words are, at best, reminders of things that have meaning, while forfeiting their own – which is another way of saying that in themselves words are meaningless. And if theirs is an arbitrary or artificially imposed connection to the things they refer to, then secondly, words never touch on reality at all, as if we're cordoned off from the world by a glass screen on which we've etched words at will, to go with the objects shimmering behind them in the distance. And what does that imply, for example, about words spoken in court? When you swear to speak the truth, the whole truth and nothing but the truth, the real truth is that your truth has to present itself in words, and words hail from a world at variance with that of objective reality. How reliable does that make your evidence? Can we, with words, ever name the truth as such, or is the most we can hope for a fist of verbal signs that are consistent with one another, and that make a working replica of the truth that looms unreachably in the hinterland? Finally, if words bear no intrinsic relation to reality, how do you secure their definitions? One answer – the one given by the Swiss linguist Ferdinand de Saussure – is that, lacking a fixed noticeboard of reality to which they might be stapled, words have to be defined in relation to each other – 'table' can be told apart from 'cable', so you know it has a slightly different meaning, and is also distinct from 'stable', 'gable' and 'fable' …

And because most books are, as we have said, made up of words, their relationship to the real world will always be a little peculiar: the separation of words from reality suggests your opting for a work either of fiction or non-fiction, say, would make little difference. Because both use language, both find themselves channelled downstream of reality. Which makes, for example, the biography of Benazir Bhutto no more authoritative than *Lolita*, for, like the Nabokov, the Bhutto book will have been restricted to trading on the outer, the merely linguistic, perimeter of the market square that entertains reality at its centre. You could even call the Nabokov the more reliable – after all, there's no one alive in possession of any facts about its heroine, being the offspring of Nabokov's imagination alone, to impugn or improve his account, whereas the Bhutto biography will, in some measure, have missed, underplayed or silenced a modicum of data, however small, that would make its portrayal more equal to the truth (a biography is never complete). Even if, as seems likely, Dolores Haze was loosely based on a real-life girl, she got transfigured into Lolita – that is, a literary character confined between the covers of a book, impregnable, as if that book were her grave, to having further characteristics assigned or any part of her falsified.

Let's say you're ready to concede that words are essentially fictitious, but not to sever all links with reality, so you decide to buy a book that hedges between the two – bearing in mind the famously gloomy German philosopher Arthur Schopenhauer's somewhat jaded caution, 'It would be a good thing to buy books if one could also buy the time to read them; but one usually confuses the purchase of books with the acquisition of their contents.' However, let's assume good intent. And so you reach for a work of 'faction', a cross between fact and fiction, such as the historical reimaginings so adroitly executed by Peter Ackroyd, and within minutes you're on the upholstered bench of a horse-drawn cab with Charles Dickens, the vapours of Victorian London nuzzling the gas-lit street lamps, the chains from a Bankside prison clanging their icy chimes through the night.

It doesn't take long before you see exactly how the line between fact and fiction seems extraordinarily blurred – not just because the book is constituted from words, which already put it at one remove from reality, but because, in this case, there's something about history which was very much like a story. Ackroyd might be embellishing the documentary record, but the facts he's describing already had something story-ish about them. For yes, the words 'story' and 'history' share the same origin, and it's hard to report the past without it taking on the properties of narrative. Even if you're just describing your last holiday, the distinction between the story and the history will inevitably melt. It's not that you'll be lying about the amazing dive you did, or the beautiful sunsets – you won't be falsifying the facts – but because, subconsciously, you'll have invested them with emotion, and given more emphasis to this rather than that, your account will contain as much story as history. When we talk about history, we should be aware that it contains this narrative element, an element that might enhance, but equally undermine, its reliability.

So much for Ackroyd's work of faction. A few chapters in, and you tire of the noisome air, the oppressive morals, the hellish swirl of cloaks, and, with your holiday in mind, you reach next for a book from sunnier climes, a south to Dickens's north, an adventure that combines with a more intense, bitter-sweet flavour the realism of fact with the magic of fiction. Not just any book, as it happens, but the book which remains the best example of the 'magic realist' genre it inaugurated, Gabriel García Márquez's *One Hundred Years of Solitude* – and you settle down.

Not that books have to be pulled from the hat of magic to feel magical. We already suspect that words are disconnected from reality and that all history is shot through with story, but, over and above those factors, any kind of reading should convey you to a world both deep inside yourself and far beyond. Even though the book is published, and so necessarily public, your experience ought to be one of sumptuous privacy, a passing through a portal into a secret land. It's a feeling captured well in the opening of *Jane Eyre*, when the young protagonist, a treasured volume in her own arms, retreats from her bothersome cousins to a window seat curtained off by 'folds of scarlet drapery': even before the book she's about to read ('Bewick's *History of British Birds*') flies her to another sphere, the act of reading itself becomes a metaphor for escape, a secular renouncing of the world. Something similar happens in the equally famous overture to Proust's *Remembrance of Things Past*: Marcel retires early to read, and as soon as he's snuffed out the candle and fallen asleep, the book he had just been reading invades his mind, so that 'it seemed to me that I myself was the immediate subject of my book'. The book becomes a flying carpet on which Marcel withdraws even further than Jane Eyre – into his own dreams.

To read any book is to imbibe the magical, therefore, but is often to take in a dose of the real, so 'magic realism' is just as suited to books that fall well outside the genre. For, just as a dossier of pure fact – the *Guinness Book of Records*, say – can take you to unimagined places, and bedazzle you with amazing feats, so a work of sheer fantasy – *Alice's Adventures in Wonderland* – constructs a universe that, no matter how surreal, assumes a logic of its own, such that the Mad Hatter or the Queen of Hearts takes on a presence, a reality, a credibility in your mind; and when the White Rabbit gets vexed about being late, you feel the urgency of his mission – after all, fictional characters have a habit of impressing themselves on your mind at least as memorably as their more boring counterparts in real life, sometimes becoming even realler to you as a result. For all the detachment of words from reality, the world of the book you're reading becomes as real as the one outside your window.

So you turn to the first page of Marquez's seminal story and start to read:

Many years later, as he faced the firing squad, Colonel Aureliano Buendía was to remember that distant afternoon when his father took him to discover ice.

But hold on a minute: what happened before you opened the book? What was the colonel doing? Was he just waiting for you, switched off like the light in the fridge before you opened it, or like a puppet that trembles into motion only when you raise it from its wooden box? Was he perhaps both dead and alive, like Schrödinger's Cat – the creature dreamed up by the atomic physicist Erwin Schrödinger to show how what you observe is affected by the fact that you observe it? To an esteemed group of scholars associated with 'Reception Theory'

– the theory of how we 'receive' texts, and thus a theory of reading – the answer is broadly that yes, the colonel didn't exist until you started reading about him. A book gets its meaning from being read, from being activated in the mind of its reader. So long as it sits on the shelf, it's a book in the sense that it has pages, covers and text, but it isn't a *book* in the full-blooded sense, the verbal aquarium of characters, colours and currents that has us entranced before it; it hasn't become itself.

In this sense, a book is like an orchestral score, with you, the reader, a conductor who teases sounds from a page that would otherwise remain mute. True, those sounds are heard only as a dumbshow in the front of your mind, never actually shattering the air to make themselves audible, but without your silent conjuring, those words would languish more silently still, dormant. However, this act of worldly resurrection on your part (a magic of its own) comes at a cost. For the words that you breathe from their papery, ghost-like state into life have, like photographic negatives, to pass through a medium, a solvent, before you can register them as such, before they become properly legible. That medium is your mind – so what, you may ask, is the problem? Well, because the book you're reading can't release any meaning without your mind to coax it out, the book suffers the same limits that you do – it can mean only as much as your mind is capable of letting it mean. Because, in other words, it's *your* mind and no one else's that does the reading, the meaning you get will be your own.

It's a situation that itself bears different interpretations. If you can't be sure that you've read the book as such – only that you've shaken the words into a meaning for you, like the pattern of tea leaves that remain in your cup – you have at least created a world that makes sense in your own terms. You've made it mean something for you, which is what, all things considered, meaning is: there's no 'meaning' in general; meaning occurs when something broad, abstract, nebulous or unfounded gets drawn down, when it switches from being a roving, sketchy monster to becoming your own pet, and one that looks like you. Which is partly why the world that you generate out of the book you're reading keeps you in isolation – and we all know the feeling of wanting to dive back into the novel we've got on the go, escaping from the people around us. Even if they're reading the very same publication, there's something special, and comforting, about our own relationship with it, which we'd prefer to keep to ourselves. On the other hand, when your feeling about a book is mirrored by another reader, there's a wonderful complicity, as if you'd both been involved in a life-changing event that no one who wasn't there would understand. Sharing an interpretation is like sharing history.

To Reception Theory, however, that's a worry. It spends a great deal of its time fretting about interpretation, or what it prefers to call 'hermeneutics' – hermeneutics as in Hermes, the most elusive of the Greek gods, the very icon of instability and movement, of zooming out of focus and into enigmatic strangeness, with riddling messages under his wing. In getting so used to associating interpretation with relativism – the idea that you're entitled to your own interpretation, that your private relationship with your book is special and there's no universally shared truth – we've somewhat forgotten why hermeneutics is important. It has its origins not in the reading of this or that book, but in the reading of *the* book, the good book, the Bible. Hermeneutics was – and in the rabbinic tradition remains – the art, the science even, of deciphering the Lord's intent through the sacred scriptures. Far from sanctioning individuals to cut out their own meanings from such precious material, the point of hermeneutics was, and to some still is, to fix very precisely the meaning – in effect, the moral purpose – contained in every phrase. Take the words 'Thou shalt not kill': if everyone were allowed their own interpretation of that commandment, where would we be?

But that raises the question of who is and isn't allowed to do the interpreting. As you press on into the first chapter of *One Hundred Years of Solitude*, where the discovery of ice one year becomes the invention of magnetism the next, no one's going to object to you taking your own meaning from it – with a work of fiction, the stakes simply aren't high enough, except in rare cases such as Salman Rushdie's *The*

Satanic Verses, interpreted by some as a slur against Mohammed, and so a work of blasphemy, punishable by death. True, the arguments in literature departments over the meaning of *Don Quixote* can get pretty heated, but, unlike some religious books, no one's going to go to war over it – it would be like tilting at windmills. For people do die as a result of their interpretation of the Bible – the persecution of the Jews, to cite an obvious example, for refusing to read the 'new testament' as the report of the Messiah's descent on to earth – which suggests conflicts take place as much between interpretations as the people who cling to them. And even though whole religions are based around such interpretations – like Jews, Muslims interpret Jesus to be a common prophet – it is typically only a chosen few who are licensed to interpret. Be it rabbi, priest or imam, when it comes to the religions of the book, an intermediary is required to interpret potentially ambiguous scriptures on behalf of the masses, and so guide those masses away from misguided thoughts. In such religious traditions, to read the book is not to be invited to the free exercise of interpretation, but to be obliged to make an obedient tracing of the truth as illuminated by the doctors of the law. Which implies a concept of the book as fundamentally encrypted, requiring the unlocking services of your neighbourhood hermeneut: some theologians go so far as to suggest that religious texts favour allegorical forms – speaking with a forked tongue – precisely to keep them esoteric, held back from the ignorant multitude. The best example of which would be the religious parable – a morality tale that can be appreciated by the simple for the tale, or by the sophisticated for the morality.

Now that we think everyone's interpretation of anything is valid, we've come a long way, and in the swinging sixties Roland Barthes, the French linguist, swung the pendulum of authority so far away from the text and its guardians, and towards the reader, that he became famous – or infamous – for announcing the 'death of the author'. For too long we readers had been browbeaten by the dictates of the books we'd read, schooled to interpret them in a narrow way that served the modern day lecturers and literati who sermonised about them. Not a million miles from Emerson – who said it was the good reader that made the good book – Barthes turned the tables on the author, saying not only that a book needs a reader to wake it into life, but that in so doing the reader becomes nothing less than the author, who revels in the book's hermeneutic possibilities, releases them and so becomes its own creator. Not that all books are quite so amenable to a reader's joyous rubbing against it – it would be pretty tough to make the telephone book, say, an object of reader's delight – and so he divided the society of books into those that were 'lisible' (readable) and the superior race of the writable, the 'scriptible'. *One Hundred Years of Solitude* would be an eminent candidate for the latter: descriptively rich, allegorically layered, a fatty, even putrid, saturation of myth with history, it provides the ideal humidity for a reader to germinate his or her own spores inside it.

So where is the author in all this? It's not unlikely that you have a favourite writer, and if you do, it suggests there's a certain style you're attracted by, a particular tone – which suggests in turn that the intellectual ownership of that writer's books is quite clear, shot through as they are, like the writing in a stick of rock, by the writer's signature. With such a pronounced style (Márquez would be a good example), there's little debate as to their authorship – it's obvious that their author was their author, not you. And just as well, really, because difference is part of the attraction – could you really become so enchanted by the books you read if every one were a reflection of yourself? Besides which, if you've ever been to a book reading by a favourite author of yours, or read an interview, or heard them on the radio, the chances are you deferred to their authority to speak about their works – it's not by accident that the words 'authority' and 'author' are connected. Despite the contraband offered you by Roland Barthes, to try on the title of writer, it seems only proper that the author is recognised as the rightful owner of the work.

Although Roland Barthes would turn in his grave to hear it, that authority is so immense that writers become gods of the universe they have created. This applies to writers of non-fiction, because, even though they are hemmed in on one side by data, by facts and reportage, they are on the other side open to recreate that empirical world in their own terms. But it applies especially to novelists, and when you read their books, they are showing you their worlds – the people they have called into existence out of thin air, the landscape they have generated, the atmosphere they have summoned and manipulated. And if we now finish by returning to the opening of *One Hundred Years of Solitude*, we'll see this all played out:

> Many years later, as he faced the firing squad, Colonel Aureliano Buendía was to remember that distant afternoon when his father took him to discover ice. At that time Macondo was a village of twenty adobe houses, built on the bank of a river of clear water that ran along a bed of polished stones, which were white and enormous, like prehistoric eggs.

These opening lines do something very clever, for they are an allegory of themselves. They describe the origins of a village as if it were Eden, the water still clear, the stones pristine, the eggs yet prehistoric, and in so doing they allude to what all books do when they begin – they create a new world for you, dear reader, to enter.

13

Watching TV

IN HIS BOOK on television, the Tasmanian writer and critic Peter Conrad says the TV is the modern-day version of the fire in the hearth, around which the family gathers. But if it's a kind of fire, it's more like the ones you see burning far away in the galaxy. For when you gaze at your TV, that furnace of pictures glowing in the corner of your room, its images combusting and folding like the gaseous explosions of a far-flung sun, you may as well be staring at a star. Television is dead, any light it emits reaching us long after its extinction, making you its final witness. Not that you won't continue to watch movies, soaps, chat shows, adverts, news, dramas, documentaries and concerts – but TV, the monopoly medium for viewing them, is over. All its content having been burgled and cloned by newer technologies, the TV, latterly a pointillist plasma sheet, will return to its origins as a box, a casket, an archive, and suffer its final ignominy of being ferried up to the attic.

But not so fast. Because there's a difference between the object it became – an everyday sphinx in your home, intercepting messages from the world beyond – and the concept on which that object was founded, the television will be survived by television itself. The clue is in the word, which means seeing ('vision') at a distance ('tele'). Even if C. P. Scott once said of this word that it's 'half Greek, half Latin – no good can come out of it', it does name something extraordinary.

For the ability to abolish distance, and so make that which is absent present, will always be a miracle, and not least because it hints at a possibility that's more amazing still: if we can beckon to our screen, to what's known as the 'haunted goldfish bowl', the six-inch-high ghosts of others, then one day we might just bring the dead back to life. Television toys with resurrection, and that's why, long after televisions themselves have seen out their half-life on waste dumps circled by seagulls, the concept of television will never be buried. The TV is dead; long live TV.

Which means, quotidian though it may be, your watching TV is a linking to eternity, its screen a window on the infinite, and in this, I'm thinking of Gilles Deleuze, the French philosopher of technology, whose ideas can be applied to this immortality at the heart of TV.

A Deleuzian argument might go as follows. If TV is about seeing things at a distance – things that happened at another time (archive footage), are happening in another place (the news), or never, save in the imagination of their author, happened at all (a movie) – those things have to be transferred to your screen as representations: they don't, as believed by the toddler who jabs his fingers against the glass, actually live inside the lucent oblong in your lounge. So TV is an art of representation – of representing people, mainly – but what is it about people that permits them to be so re-presented? Imagine you were the eyewitness to a lunchtime bank robbery, and that afternoon a gaggle of TV journalists flocks to interview you for the evening news – which, once back at home, you switch on with interest. What allows you simultaneously to speak on the screen and sit on the sofa is the fact that you could be split off from yourself, or – to use Deleuze's terms – made different from yourself, with one of you watching the show on which the other you is talking. That implies, obviously enough, that even as you were giving the interview, part of you was capable of being transmitted to thousands of TVs, of becoming detached from yourself for broadcast, of allowing yourself to be multiplied for myriad screens around the nation. Which implies in turn – and here's the punchline – that in the throes of being recorded, you weren't exclusively there:

yes, you stood before mike and camera, fielding questions, but at the same time you were silently absenting yourself, posting yourself into the camera that was capturing your talking head for a million reproductions of it. Had you been absolutely present to the moment of recording, utterly absorbed in the now of it, there couldn't have been any later of it – the present would have sizzled all your presence up, with nothing left for the viewers at home. To record someone for TV is to exploit this blip in our otherwise unbroken occupation of any given moment in time; it's because, in the instant, we can't be perfectly in attendance that we can be represented. The upshot is that when you watch people on TV, you are observing immortals – not because the programme might get repeated, or because you could watch them even after they've died (both true), but because, while the recording light was red, they were surviving themselves, self-duplicating as efficiently as a species facing extermination.

In the words of Wim Wenders, exponent, along with such luminaries as Reiner Werner Fassbinder and Werner Herzog, of the New German Cinema, the camera thus provides 'a weapon against the misery of things – namely, their disappearance'. The camera and immortality go hand in hand. Except that Wenders is referring to cinema rather than TV, so what's the difference? Of course, TV can include films, just as it can include numberless other genres, and this is part of its point. 'Watching TV' means watching the world go by, and affirming – even when you jib at the sex, the shooting, the starving – the polymorphous perversity of life. It's this embracing of the empirical that sets TV apart from the hypothetic, bracketed mode of the film, at least when that film is played in a cinema. Emphasised by its shoebox darkness, the film in the cinema turns away from the world, whereas the TV, which you watch with the lights on, doesn't pretend not to be part of everyday life. Even when you're watching an arthouse film on your set, the fact that you can get up to fix a drink or answer the phone breaks the illusion of being at a remove from reality, the illusion created in the cinema.

But just because TV is so embedded in the world, this doesn't mean its relationship to that world is always straightforward. On which subject, it's worth drawing on the ideas of two distinguished thinkers who consider all forms of 'cultural production', like TV, as ideologically motivated. The first is the Welsh Marxist Raymond Williams, for whom cultural products both reflect and debunk the culture they spring from.

For example, *Sex and the City*, starring Sarah Jessica Parker as the leader of a BCBG gang of ladies – a group of bourgeois thirty-somethings – pursuing personalised forms of happiness in upwardly mobile Manhattan. It came too late for Williams himself to tackle as a subject, but there's no doubting that the show celebrated the values of the society it came out of, those of capitalistic consumption: of shopping (what cute shoes!), of dating (what cute guys!), even of friendship (what great girls!), each of which made for an essential luxury, where 'essential' and 'luxury' were not, as in old money they would be, in opposition. As if going back to seventies feminism, but decoupling it from feminism's socialist instincts, the girls created a lifestyle that merged the best of both worlds – that is, both sexual emancipation and money. And so it turned its back on economic inconvenience, arguing that a girl's satisfaction could be derived from spending, insured by the low-resolution but high-net-worth males who occasionally appeared – which turned the 'women' into children licensed to behave like candy-floss Cinderellas. Somewhere, remotely, serious money was being made, but not by these ladies, who, like modern-day plantation dames, simply lunched on the back of it.

Utterly reprehensible, no? Well, no. Only at one level was *Sex and the City* this confident transmission of bourgeois codes for you, the viewer, to install into your own outlook on life. For Williams, the workings of ideology are rarely so simple. Granted, the unironic delight in consumerism made it seem as though, if one of the show's parents was the sitcom, the other was the advert – as if the characters might leak into the commercial breaks to do a bit of shopping, before sneaking back on set. But that acquisitive drive for Hermès handbags and handsome hunks was never permitted to overtop the power of the sorority itself – the four coming together for the ritual brunch – which served, in its own right, as a forum for analysing the very culture that provoked so irresistibly the desire to shop. More than grown-up girl power, this was in fact a post-feminist feminism, the women comparing notes on how to negotiate the snakes and ladders on New York City's grid; on the modernity with which it confronted them; and on the prevailing atmosphere of competition that threatened to undo their makeshift solidarity.

In other words, television might reflect society, but it also responds to it, such that to watch TV is to be both trapped in that society and offered the password for escape; when commentators claim that violence on TV leads to violence on the streets, the argument can be reversed: violence on TV might be a way of processing what's going on in the outside world. Marshall McLuhan, however, writing at the same time as Williams but on the other side of the Atlantic, allowed for less redemption. To McLuhan, sitting in front of *Sex and the City* would be no different from catching a quiz show or the weather forecast, for, across the board, the primary purpose of the content is to distract you from the form. 'Societies have always been shaped more by the nature of the media by which men communicate than by the content of the communication,' says McLuhan, who goes on to talk about how the alphabet, as an example, conditions the way we think. The twenty-six letters constitute not a natural but a man-made system whose artificiality we no longer notice, but which determines the words we make, and thus the ideas we can have: if we have no word, say, for something that is both true and false, it's not because no such phenomenon exists, it's because the English dictionary simply doesn't list it, and so we're unlikely to consider the possibility. The medium rules, hence McLuhan's slogan that 'the medium is the message' – or, in later versions, the medium is the *massage*. Either way, you, the hapless viewer, are, like a slowly boiled frog, being cooked into blissful unawareness of the medium you're staring it. For the truth is that when you 'watch television', you're not watching *television*, you're watching this or that show, and if a synonym for 'entertainment' is 'diversion', that is exactly right: glued to the whodunit, you lose the larger plot. Were you to watch the medium itself, you might be more alert to the ways you're being controlled.

McLuhan's views lie not a million miles away, of course, from those of George Orwell, for whom TV was a kind of pacifier. While the news might raise your hackles, a rom-com make you weep and a baseball game have you punching the ceiling, the overriding function of television might be simply to keep you watching, to detonate your energy safely within your living room, rather than letting you take your chances with the political hurly-burly of the street. Instead of you watching it, that would make the TV screen, in a sinister swivelling around of its role, more like a surveillance camera watching you, like the moving eyes in an ancestor's portrait, or the telescreens in *Nineteen Eighty-Four*. But whether it's watching you or not, you'll find it hard not to watch it, and we've all been in bars or airports where, try as we might not to peek, our eye keeps being drawn back to the screen. So the real question is 'What makes the screen so mesmerising?' Considering that most of us can walk, talk, have relationships and play games, why do we find ourselves – and by no means always reluctantly – so fixated on this radiant panel before our eyes? Could it be because the screen is the home of images, and images

a) are *intrinsically* more compelling than other media? Communications professionals love to assert that 80 per cent of communication is visual, and if you're sitting through a lecture, say, which is not only verbal but one-way, you'll retain 20 per cent at most. There are various precursors to TV – picture books, zoetropes, cinema itself – but you could argue it goes right back to the church's stained-glass windows. Faced with a largely illiterate congregation, but with a mission to impress on them certain principles, what better medium than dramatic pictures in lurid, transparent colours telling stories of personal salvation? Without the extra tissue of words to muffle the effect, the images, burning through the tracery of lead, could be branded on to the soul direct.

b) excite desire? If our inner fantasies come more in images than in words or sounds, it would be the screen rather than the radio, say, that would provide their more natural home in the external world. In other words, TV is more likely either to reproduce your own inner garden of visual delights or to produce images that you might smuggle back into that garden for your private enjoyment.

c) present themselves in a rhythm that rhymes with your own? If there is this affinity, or even an identity, between your inner images and those on the TV screen, the task of producing those images might conceivably be shared between you and it. Syncing so well with that inner landscape, TV images might relieve you of some psychic labour, as if working your REM cycle on your behalf.

All this talk of images, however, overlooks the fact that you don't just watch when you watch TV, you also listen. It's after all *audio*-visual, and if you were to take away the audio, you'd be left with something less than TV. Key to this is the anchor voice, the voice that segues between programmes, or the voice that reads the news – where the news voice effectively works as the voice of the TV itself. While the images it punctuates can be extreme, this archetypal TV voice is nearly always 'normal', vernacular, neutral, unthreatening, even classless, and it's this tone of the TV voice which belongs to a larger democratic project. By making itself as neutral as possible, that voice is trying not to get in the way of what you watch, and so reinforces the role of TV in general, which involves handing back the robes of judgement to the viewer, the court assembled in armchairs, to pass comment on what it sees. For the closest relative that TV has among other machines is not the cinema projector or computer, but the poly-graph, aka the lie detector. To watch TV is to be given the chance to assess the veracity, the integrity, the sincerity of what you're watching, and even when there's no sound at all, you are likely still to be reaching for a verdict. In fact, having the sound turned down can make that job of appraisal more focused: without the distracting decibels, you can home in on the inaudible signs – the 'tells' or 'reveals' such as pursed lips, prolonged blinks, beads of sweat – in a programme of either fact or fiction that give the villain away. And because, like a kangaroo court, there's no comeback from the people on screen, no stricture on you to prove your case, you can indulge in the self-affirming pleasures of unchallenged opinion.

Of course, much of this applies to watching things at the cinema – the difference is that, the cinema's sealed-off space inhibits the kind of raucous commentary that the TV allows or even encourages. Where cinema means being private in public, TV means being public in private. So if it's democracy, if it's popular justice, watching TV is a pretty seedy, banana-republic variety. Like overweight fans barking at fullbacks to run faster down the wing, TV audiences enjoy all the authority of judgement with none of the responsibility that a mature democracy would append. Which is precisely why watching TV is so alluring. Small wonder that the few whose job it is to review TV incite envy: because of this lack of responsibility, watching TV can't seriously be work, can it? The essence of laziness, you're not only encouraged to pass judgement on others, you can even do it with your feet up, your defrosted dinner on a tray and a chilled beer at your side.

The whole, comforting and comfortable activity comes together in the remote control – the indispensable gadget of modern living. From the era of the Flintstones, and probably long before, what's set the human species apart is its intelligence, where intelligence is the ability to overcome natural limitations by employing other means that are near to hand – a rock to bash in a coconut, a strip of bark to swat a mosquito, a bunch of palm fronds to sweep ashes from the floor. And although each of those materials – stone, wood, leaf – is natural in itself, it becomes, when deployed as an adjunct to the human's own natural state, something opposite to nature: it becomes a tool, a technology. But it's not just that those technologies supplement the human in his or her industry – in their efficiency, they outstrip the human productivity rate that, in executing the same task, would have taken twice as long. To control something remotely, even in the digital age, is to continue this logic of leverage, of securing disproportionate return on effort invested; and the ratio of investment to return is nowhere greater than in the TV remote, which, with a mere flinch of the muscles in the thumb, can spin a whole planet's activity in front of your eyes and motionless body.

If intelligence itself is natural to the human, and intelligence means, among other things, creating and exploiting technologies, then using a remote is in its own way a completely natural activity, one that expresses the human being's ancient, innate connection with things technical. Better therefore to think of the remote less as a gizmo than as a prosthesis, a literal extension of the hand, that completes an action human beings had instigated millions of years ago. That would make watching TV not a guilty pleasure, a sluicing through the dumbed-down sink of recycled images, but a reminder of the technical mastery that began with the origin of the species. So lie back and tune in – watching TV proves just how smart you are.

14

Cooking and eating dinner

WITH THE POSSIBLE EXCEPTION of Esperanto, all languages contain impurities, each the product of invasion, innovation, cross-breeding and accident. None more so than English, a dog's break-fast of Anglo-Saxon, German, Latin, Greek and French, let alone its random borrowings from elsewhere: 'checkmate' (Persian for 'the king is dead'), 'palaver' (from the Portuguese '*palavra*', meaning 'word') or 'char' (from the Chinese word for tea). Fitting, then, that the founda-tion stone of English literature is taken to be the verse epic *Beowulf* – which isn't really in English, features a Swedish warrior and is set in Denmark.

Written by an author now unknown, at a date also lost to the Dark Ages, the recessive mystery of the text's origin is paralleled in its subject matter. In an atmosphere of unpredictable threat, where nothing is certain except uncertainty itself, the eponymous hero does battle with a creature who, long before DC Comics invented Swamp Thing, was its prototype: a gruesome amphibian called Grendel, who from the wintry gloom rises, fangs forward, to lay siege to Beowulf and his doughty comrades. Amidst such gothic grimness, this glacier of a work describes the struggle between the nascent civilisation of the warriors, as expressed in their traditions, and the rebarbative, retard-ing and retaliatory effects of nature, embodied by the fiend. Which as dramaturgy isn't so remarkable, except that it all comes down to eating.

Grendel, whose very name sounds like delight in the grinding of molars, is a demon of carnivorous hunger. Here's one of his more typical mealtimes:

Straightway he seized a sleeping warrior
for the first, and tore him fiercely asunder,
the bone-frame bit, drank blood in streams,
swallowed him piecemeal …

As Richard Dreyfuss's character says of the shark in *Jaws*, Grendel is a perfect eating-machine, and, like the famous fin, functions as a measure of his prey's valour; the only difference is that where the scourge of Amity Island operates in silence and by stealth, the dastardly griffin is a rampager of the highest volume. But if the monster is constitutionally man-eating, so the men who constitute his diet are defined by feasting at the mead-hall, which is the epicentre of their universe: when not relating their own descent and derring-do, the men are either eating or being eaten. For eating, and the ritual that attends it within the refectory that glints like a jewel in the blackness, is the marker of their culture, a statement of their society's beauty as slavered over by the beast. In coming together to sup, they are affirming mutual belonging in the face of an adversary that threatens to wrench that culture from them and stamp on it. If for Grendel eating is about power, for the men it's about identity – the reaching, at the risk of having their backsides bitten by the demon, for the highest point on the food chain.

This goes to the ambivalence at the heart of eating – does it signal barbarism or civilisation? Are you, when you tuck in to your chicken escalope, exposing your animal origins or, on the contrary, demonstrating how far you've left them behind? In answering the question, you might turn to *The Raw and the Cooked*, the celebrated work of French anthropologist Claude Lévi-Strauss, which argues it's not the eating that determines how civilised you are, but the cooking and, in particular, whether you cook the food at all. While the raw is associated with savagery, primitivism and violence, the cooked represents the opposite – civilisation, sophistication and social intercourse. It's a schema *Beowulf* plays out neatly, with Grendel – and his yet more rapacious hag of a mother – preferring the men uncooked, while the men, confirming their superiority, choose the hot option. When you, in turn, cook dinner, you're not just transforming raw ingredients with heat, you are showing how humans have been culturally cooked – and how far you yourself have overcome the rawness you were born with.

To Lévi-Strauss, whole cultures operate on such binary structures – giving and taking, friend and foe, sacred and profane – the raw/cooked pair holding particular weight because it defines the difference between cultured cultures and those that are still 'backward' – which effectively means it defines culture per se. And if for this, his insistence on the structuring power of such opposites, Lévi-Strauss was known as a 'structuralist', it's not that he thought societies *develop* such structures; it's more the other way round: somewhat like laws, only more primary, structures determine societies. The brethren of *Beowulf* weren't the authors of their modus vivendi – it's rather that the archetypal polarity of raw and cooked gave the warriors the idea, albeit subconsciously, that there was a choice between them. They then aligned themselves with the 'cooked' side of the equation, and with that alignment came a sense of identity. It's not unlike how people might choose their politics: until you know there's a choice between left and right wing, you're not sure where your sympathies will lie; but once you know, you make a choice and then you identify yourself as a person as either conservative or liberal. As long as the warriors keep feasting, and monsters keep baying for their blood, their cosmos remains in order.

While such structures furnish the eager anthropologist with a passe-partout for unlocking otherwise impenetrable societies, they're not unambiguous. For a start, the raw and the cooked are not pure opposites – a boiled carrot is the same carrot it was when raw; even as it's transformed by cooking, its nature persists. But nor can the raw and the cooked be coupled without a third term – the rotten

– infecting them. For although there are plenty of cultural prohibitions on what you can eat – meat forbidden on religious grounds (pork or beef), alcohol reserved for the initiated (Manischewitz or Communion wine) and any sole entitlement of the monarch (venison, in the past, or swan) – rottenness, because it's natural, sets a more decisive boundary. Whether or not you cook something that's raw, it will eventually go off and its rottenness will be pretty much the opposite of culture.

Or will it? 'Rottenness' is capable of a refinement of its own, nowhere more obvious than in the name of the German wine Noble Rot, whose grapes are harvested at so belated a point they've been affected by fungus. In the game of culture, a degree of putrefaction – the long-hung grouse, the festering Camembert, the turning durian – can trump the merely well done, because while the raw and the cooked present worthy categories for the anthropologist, the rotten belongs to the aesthete. To cite the words of Anthelme Brillat-Savarin, to whom we'll return at the end of the chapter: 'The desirable stage is reached just as the pheasant begins to decompose.' Sometimes, not ripeness but overripeness is all, and may speak better of your taste.

'Taste' being in this context, a loaded word. Cooking and eating dinner, of course, involve taste in both senses, and as well as Lévi-Strauss one might on this topic briefly consult his compatriot, Pierre Bourdieu who himself rose from humble origins as the son of a postman, to become one of the grandest academics on the French scene. Concerned mainly with the purpose that cultural activities serve, Bourdieu argues that 'taste' has little to do with what it's usually defined as – the ability to make insightful choices in aesthetic matters. If, when preparing a salad, you opt to make your dressing not with supermarket vinegar but with the cave-aged balsamic vinegar you picked up from a small estate near Modena, it's not that you're that much more discerning. No, you're merely asserting your level of 'distinction' – that is, drawing a class difference, and confirming that you belong in a certain social category which, in ways that matter to you, you consider superior.

And the cave-aged vinegar example, though not Bourdieu's, is telling, because again it suggests that being 'cultured' often involves choosing things to eat that are, if not actually rotten, at least in an advanced state of maturation. Conceivably, such choices correspond with what Edward Said, distinguished critic of Western culture, termed 'late style', the phenomenon whereby the artwork produced in the mature years of its creator's life acquires a depth, a subtlety that not only exceeds that of the youthful works but approaches the sublime. Be it Beethoven's *Große Fugue in B flat major*, which Said discusses, or a vintage Château d'Yquem, 'lateness' means it has achieved an unprecedented complexity which, instead of confusing, intensifies its identity.

Despite all such arguments, however, this aesthetics of supersaturated maturity still has an equally convincing opposite: to not cook at all, but offer up the raw can just as nicely demonstrate your grade of cultivation. It's hinted at in the idea of serving meat pink, becomes more obvious in ceviche (whereby raw scallops or tuna, say, are 'cured' in lime juice) and is completely explicit in the Pacific oyster, yellowtail sashimi, Beluga caviar, ostrich carpaccio or lamb tartare – none of which requires much preparation beyond being dressed on a plate. In these cases, it's in the not-cooking that the sophistication lies – and, if you can procure the ingredients, such would be the way to lay on a dinner party of minimum effort, maximum impact. While landmark restaurants like El Bulli and The Fat Duck pride themselves on alimentary conceits featuring leather, liquid nitrogen and paint extracted from pistachio, these days Michelin stars go as much to ingredients in their unadorned state – the Maine lobster poached with baby broad beans served raw from the kitchen garden, or the Kobe beef grilled with just gratings of fresh horseradish on the side.

That said, the sophistication it takes to serve and eat raw matter never throws quite enough of the starched linen over its potential for horror. This isn't to say there aren't horrors associated with other cooked food, like veal, whose pale flush depends on the claustrophobic confinement of the calf in a crate; foie gras, which requires the forced bloating of the goose's liver; and especially the persecuted ortolan. This was the illicit and indeed illegal amuse-bouche that featured in François Mitterrand's last supper – illegal because both preparation and consumption call for an almost Aztec cruelty. The ortolan – a bunting, the size of a sparrow – is trapped and incarcerated in a windowless box, to be fed figs; when it has fattened, it is literally drowned in Armagnac, its minute lungs flooded with the rasping liquor. Now dead, it is plucked, roasted and served whole – bones, guts, pluck and all – with only the head to be left dangling untouched beyond its eater's lips. So barbaric is the practice that diners do indeed try to conceal it, each taking a napkin that covers not just the chest, as would a bib, but the entire head, like a hood – thus hiding the shameful crunching and swallowing not just from each other, but from the judging eyes of God. All of which suggests that, just as either the overripeness or the rawness of what you serve can speak to your cultivation, to your acquired level of artistry, so cruelty can exhibit your refinement. In all cases, what matters is taking up an extreme position, standing at a corner of the triangle – raw, rotten or ruthless – to show how you've retreated from the peasants in its middle, who've made much blander choices.

In cannibalism, however, such extremities of sophistication meet – with some notable exceptions – their limit. One such exception would be *The Cook, The Thief, His Wife and Her Lover*, the film in which a gluttonous gangster bullies a bookish rival for his wife's love. While the gangster gorges himself on ever more fancy dishes at his favourite eatery, wife and rival, in a pun on 'intercourse', do it in the toilets. Inevitably, everything goes sour: husband murders rival by jamming books down his throat – forcing him, in another pun, to eat his words – only for the wife to compel the husband to eat the lover's body, roasted to perfection by the restaurant's accomplished chef. You'll note that gangster and academic represent opposing ends of that eating spectrum from barbarity to civilisation, and yet, in the bathroom cubicle that itself resembles a stable, the more civilised coupling of wife and lover reveals, in part, their animal nature – revealed in full when the lover is glazed and served exactly like a roast pig. With the climax of this revenge tragedy, the wife therefore consummates the gastro-erotic journey her husband had initiated by serving the ultimate delicacy and breaking – we're way beyond ortolans here – the final taboo.

Although Peter Greenaway's film has a counterpart in *The Silence of the Lambs*, in which Hannibal 'the Cannibal' Lecter balances his own barbarism with the wit to serve human liver with 'a very fine Chianti', typically, the eating *by* the human *of* the human is considered the most depraved act of all, the perdition of human grace. Even in the marooned lifeboat, this option-which-isn't-an-option of turning on the weakest for their flesh can never be implemented without the survivor's enduring guilt and a wound left on his own humanity, a sin that might forever remain indigestible; even in Cormac McCarthy's *The Road*, the one line of civility in a civilisation laid waste is that dividing those who, in their famished desperation, do and don't eat other people. For the Lévi-Straussian, cannibalism even sits on a par with incest, but not, as you might expect, on moral grounds: just as you can't reproduce from your own family without foreclosing its economic expansion or breeding deformity into it, so cannibalism is a short-sighted fix that reduces available capacity and, in the long run, defeats the human race – which makes incest and cannibalism the species-level versions of suicide, or what you might call sui-genocide. Again, it's the structural point that counts: regardless of the morals, cannibalism is a self-limiting practice which will see societies wither.

All this talk of the carnal, however, will surely disturb the vegetarian, and if you're someone who prefers lentils to lamb, tofu to T-bone, you might beg to differ. While the world's most famous vegetarian was that apogee of bloodlust Adolf Hitler, it was his political antithesis from a century before, the revolutionary Romantic, Percy Bysshe Shelley, who has been the vegetarian's most eloquent apologist:

It is evident that those who ... trifle with the sacredness of life, and think lightly of the agonies of living beings, are unfit for the benevolence and justice which is required for the performance of the offices of civilised society. They are by necessity brutal, coarse, turbulent and sanguinary. Their habits form an admirable apprenticeship to the more wasting wickedness of war, in which men are hired to mangle and murder their fellow beings by thousands, that tyrants and countries may profit. How can he be expected to preserve a vivid sensibility to the benevolent sympathies of our nature, who is familiar with carnage, agony and groans? The very sight of animals in the fields who are destined to the axe must encourage obduracy if it fails to awaken compassion. The butchering of harmless animals cannot fail to produce much of that spirit of insane and hideous exultation in which news of a victory is related altho' purchased by the massacre of a hundred thousand men.

In appealing to the 'sacredness of life', Shelley, who was expelled from university for atheism, adapts a religious belief, held mainly by Hindus and Buddhists, that an animal is blessed with a soul, a belief that prepared the ground for the more recent view that it enjoys rights. In both cases, the animal possesses intangible and innate assets of which it ought never be deprived, and especially not by humans, whose assets are only the same. Which is to say that killing an animal is an internecine act, hence the continuum Shelley has in mind that leads from the culling of animals to the killing of humans. But despite this approximate parity between human and animal, Shelley is marginally keener to protect the former. It's the potential encroachment upon other humans of the human's violence towards beasts that makes his polemic not just vegetarian but – and here is the key contrast with the Führer – pacifist. The message is that animals are noble, and cooking meat makes you beastly – that is, more animal than the animal.

But whether meat or veg or both, there's little supper to sing for unless you submit them to a certain cooking method, and in this there's an increasingly polarised choice between carton and Cordon Bleu. While the 'ring or ping' culture (ring of pizza guy, ping of microwave) has burgeoned, its logical extension the cosmonaut's meal-in-a-tablet, there's a corresponding resurgence in cooking at home; of the hitherto professional spaces that have, through wiki and blog, been opened up to the amateur, one is the kitchen, where the domestic cook is invited to emulate the gourmet. Much resides in the technical – chopping an onion without splicing the root, emulsifying egg with oil so it doesn't split, roasting the cloves before pummelling – but it's more about the philosophy. Devoted cooks often describe their culinary preparations as 'therapeutic', and in doing so tap into traditions of contemplative life as ancient as the monastic habits of cultivating the herbarium, brewing beer and paring fresh produce in communal silence. In a certain sense, cooking *is* philosophy, either because, while you're scraping the squash, you'll use the time for reflection or because your dissecting of the pepper, your boning of the chicken, your filleting of the mackerel will present the anatomy of things, disclose their inner workings, for you to note and probe. This analytic quality to preparing ingredients then carries over into the cooking itself, which, like philosophy, is the transforming of the half-intuited into the fully conceived, a working over and a making digestible for others. In becoming a dish, your ingredients are given meaning; when you cook dinner, you run the gamut from opening them up with surgical coolness to recombining them through heating, and in the process you articulate and redefine their relationship with each other, as if they were concepts in search of a thesis.

It's a line of thinking that goes back to the early nineteenth century of Brillat-Savarin's *The Philosopher in the Kitchen*, where cooking and philosophy are combined as satisfyingly as peaches and cream. As it happens, his last chapter describes 'A day with the monks of St Bernard'. But perhaps the last word here should go to fish, the eating of which is known to improve the brain, and to which Brillat-Savarin devotes the following 'Philosophical Reflection':

Fish, taken collectively in all their species, offer the philosopher an endless source of meditation and surprise.

The various forms of these strange creatures, the senses which they lack, the limited powers of those which they possess, the influence on their habit of the element in which they live and breathe and move, all combine to extend the range of our ideas, and our understanding of the infinite modifications which may arise from matter, movement and life.

For my part, I look upon them with a feeling akin to respect, born of the conviction that they are antediluvian creatures; for the vast cataclysm which drowned our great-uncles about eight hundred years after the creation of the world was a time of joy, conquest and great festivity for the fishes.

15

Going to a party

Nobody knows where my Johnny has gone,
But Judy left the same time …
Why was he holding her hand
When he's supposed to be mine?

THAT'S THE FIRST VERSE of 'It's My Party', the hit from 1963 produced by the prodigious Quincy Jones. Short and sweet though it is – and self-consciously naïve, if that's not a contradiction in terms – it contains an entire philosophy, psychology and politics.

Clearly, the party hasn't gone to plan. The singer – let's call her Lesley, after the recording artist, Lesley Gore, who first made the tune famous – has asked boyfriend Johnny to her party, only for him to vanish with Judy, who, having also been invited, must be a friend. Betrayal most foul is the subject of the song, with lonesome Lesley, in a double whammy, humiliated by not one but two people – two people, moreover, she might have expected to trust. So Judy and Johnny injure the relationship with Lesley, even if they now have one with each other: hand in hand, they forge a fresh bond (the joining of hands, whether a handshake or the intertwining of lovers' fingers, being trust's most enduring symbol). Thanks to the arithmetic of love that three divided by two leaves one left over, the new pair must displace the old, leaving Lesley behind, the centre of the party shunted into the wings, sacrificed to the romantic ambitions of two hitherto valued peers. In a moment we'll examine such Machiavellian behaviour with Machiavelli himself, and look at the politics of friendship as described by Montaigne; but first, a word about Lesley's consternation and grief, about crying at your own party.

If her hopes have been dashed and her plans for the party gone awry, it's due not wholly to the selfish intentions of the furtive new incumbents. For a start, Johnny and Judy have only, like Johnny and Lesley before them, become enthralled to a force of union more powerful than either of their young hearts. Implicit, perhaps, in Lesley's shock at their heinous crime is the understanding that the tide of love flows fast and fickle, that it can carry people off at whim, stronger than their efforts to resist. More shocking still, by throwing the party in the first place, Lesley herself made the rushing in of that tide more likely: a party swings its doors open to an unpredictable current, its guests prone to getting caught up in the confusion of possibilities, in novel connections or strange combinations, and alluring eddies that cause them to circle one another in social or sexual enquiry.

In other words, the party goes wrong because the god of parties sits not – to use the grand division passed down from the ancient Greeks – on the throne of necessity but of chance. Which is part of the point. Going to a party means having the normal rules suspended, breaking away from routine, embarking on an evening's adventure where not everything will be programmed in advance. This isn't to say that, in the form of protocol, parties don't have necessities of their own – what to wear, when to arrive, what to bring, when to leave – but that, above and beyond such immediate etiquette, the spirit of the party asks that those rules be relaxed, allowing chance to be welcomed in across the threshold. A loosening up must be permitted, a melting down of the timetable that encases the weekdays and workdays, or else the party becomes a pain; and when, on occasion, the stipulations do stifle the spirit – the wedding bash where the seating plan inhibits the fun and a limp corsage can spoil the show – the party degrades into a series of tasks to grin and grind through. The sorriest example must be the corporate do, funded by the marketing department and performed in the soulless name of networking, its climax arriving, like a singles party, with the exchange of numbers, its end not love but money.

Yet even there, amid the typed-up name badges, that spirit of random encounter prevails, the coming together between people that couldn't have been perfectly plotted – exactly what poor Lesley falls victim to. You can imagine her imagining the party in the days running up to it, directing the party-goers like actors in her head, dancing with Johnny to the envy of her girl friends, and fatally failing to take into account just how much the genie of partying smiles on the unsolicited encounter, the recombination of persons, the Brownian motion of bodies, the swirling of human curiosity, all conspiring against her best-laid plans. Of tears it is said that they count among the few biological functions without evolutionary explanation – except for crocodile tears, faked to gain advantage, they constitute pure, contentless expression; the tears that Lesley cries are the secretions of chance, of her blindness to its aberrancy, and they wash her adolescent eyes with stinging hindsight. Where hosting the party should have given her more, not less, control over events, Lesley finds herself outflanked by fortune, a result she tries to part-redeem with pathos: while she can't legislate for the actions of cad Johnny or cow Judy, the fact that she's the host means she has more licence than would another guest in how to respond. The tears are her defiant, ironic way of cashing in that allowance, that prerogative of hosting: it's her party and she'll cry if she wants to.

Her blubbing might be understandable (you would cry too if it happened to you), but lachrymose Lesley is, in Machiavellian terms, a disgrace. Allowing herself to fall victim to fortune and its playing out in the machinations of members of her inner circle was bad enough, but having her own status so publicly undermined is, as we'll see, unforgivable. You might say that's unfair – that, for their disloyalty, the blame should go on Judy and Johnny – but in Machiavelli's book, it's with Lesley that the buck must stop. The only thing she did right, in fact, was to conceive the party as an opportunity to display her symbolic capital as embodied in the relationship with Johnny. That was praiseworthy because, had she been able to see it through, Lesley's position would have been shored up, the alliance with Johnny building her social range and influence, and so reducing the vulnerability natural to this young maiden. Beyond that flash of strategic insight, Lesley lost it. Don't be fooled that a party can ever be the ingenuous exercise of fun, Machiavelli might say, because, just as there's no such thing as a free lunch, there's no party without politics, no way you can bring together people with overlapping interests without a degree of tension vibrating through the room.

Although a seasoned diplomat in his own right, and therefore more than au fait with the niceties of social events, Machiavelli never wrote about parties per se, but his famous tract, *The Prince*, offers a guide on maintaining your position in a socio-political environment, of which a party is the perfect microcosm. You could even say that, if Machiavelli's locus of interest is the prince's court, the party represents a courtly dance, with Lesley in this case cast as its princess, the queen of the party who falls from a royal highness to the all-too-human depths of dejection. Had she read her Machiavelli, she'd know the pre-eminent task of any princess is what he calls '*mantenere lo stato*' – that is, to defend your status and keep your position intact – for when, like a prince, you're at the top, the only way is down. In putting on a party, that's the objective Machiavelli would counsel you to prioritise, and it demands you shake off any childish belief that parties are a frippery, little more than a purposeless hedonism that carries on outside political time, or that they occupy a niche carved out from daily life for an idle review of it. For rather than being peripheral to the week's work, they provide its anchor.

Think, for example, of the opening scenes of that film which practically announces itself as a direct heir of Machiavelli, *The Godfather*: while the party whoops and skirls beyond the shuttered interior, Don Corleone and consigliere transact their shady business, and there's no doubt where the party has its true centre. The dancing and singing function primarily as a decoy from the main event happening in this inner sanctum – only we, the viewers, are ushered in to witness the underbelly, to glimpse the politics taking place in the dark, which countersign the frivolities in the flashing sunlight outside. The party, far from imposing a light interlude between the heavy matters of business, lets the godfather, like a dictator at a military fly-past, display his social and political hardware. The tragedy for Lesley is that she too had tried to show off her wares, but instead of being there in the back room to intervene when Judy and Johnny were setting to business of their own, she found herself stranded out on the dance floor.

The point about this behind-the-scenes brokering at a party is not so much that the margins make up the middle, that the side conversations – in the kitchen, by the flowerbed, on the balcony – form the centre of the action, but that by squaring people off in this way – talking to them off-line – you can bring fortune under your command, or at least reduce the likelihood of its stochastic effects scotching your ambitions. The party's compact with chance means you'll only ever tame it so much, but at least, like a Machiavellian diplomat, you can say, in order to secure your eminence, you truly worked the room, and those leading off it. More troubling is that, in the politics of the party, friendship itself is no less vulnerable to the same unravelling. It's a sentiment as associated with the Mafia as Machiavelli, of course, that you should keep your friends close but your enemies closer, and that implies there's no such thing as genuine friendship at all – none who can't become grist to your political mill. However, the essence of friendship should be a rejection of politicking, the withstanding of caprice – it's the reason Lesley could never again be friends with Judy and Johnny, who let caprice be their wandering star – and a remaining loyal. As the togetherness of friends, a party has therefore, despite Machiavelli, to be a celebration of the fidelity among equals, of the bond of true friendship that doesn't allow itself to be broken by a better offer. Because it calls a halt to hierarchies that obtain during work, the party becomes, like friendship, a great leveller: if only one definition of friendship were allowed, it would be the one to which Aristotle refers, that neither friend in a friendship may be better than the other – which is why the relationship between friends so often borrows its model from that between brothers or sisters, who know too much about each other to act superior for very long.

Going to a party, then, means you agree to be taken on your personal merits, that you will rely neither on pulling rank nor on being obsequious – that you come in friendship, and that you *take part*, where the sense of the word 'party' is exactly that – a becoming party to something, a joining in in such a way that you leave any pretensions to or concerns about status at the door. Graphically, that would make the line of a party a horizontal rather than a vertical: Lesley's party nosedives when it flips from the former to the latter; where all was equilibrium, she suddenly discovers Judy and Johnny in ascendance and herself cast down. For as soon as someone gets bested by someone else, both party and friendship are damaged, and a ladder of differences symbolically erects itself. You can detect it even in Machiavelli's famous admonition that it's 'better to be feared than loved': as ever, Machiavelli's concern for the prince is that he maintain his '*stato*', and whereas love involves the mutual gaze of equals, fear will promote you to a higher echelon, with your so-called friends on the rungs below, propping you up.

This might contain a philosophy of friendship, but it's hardly a friendly philosophy, and as if in rebuttal of this Machiavellian view of the world Montaigne, also a courtier, wrote a century later that:

> Within a fellowship the peak of perfection consists in friendship, for all forms of it which are forged or fostered by pleasure or profit or by public or private necessity are so much the less beautiful and noble – and therefore so much the less 'friendship' – in that they bring in some purpose, end or fruition other than the friendship itself.

It's precisely because friendship seeks no purpose that it becomes ennobled, and for Montaigne friendship has the potential to become one of the loftiest experiences of all. Whenever you recruit friends to some 'purpose, end or fruition other than the friendship itself', you're not making friends but hiring accomplices – and again, that's why friends and parties go together like cheese and wine. Going to a party should be an end in itself, not a means of personal advancement, and so while Judy and Johnny, by embracing each other, embrace the party's spirit of chance, they fail its second criterion – that you don't use the event to gain advantage over others (especially not your host; at the very least, they should have waited until the party was over). That Lesley gets swept so brusquely aside means her rival and her lover, in cahoots, have misused her party as a vehicle for their own 'fruition'.

What an excellent word for a party. You shouldn't use them to further your own agenda – sucking up to this film director for a part, that magazine editor for a job – but parties have a seductive or erotic ambition of their own that can only make 'fruition' – which we'll redefine as, say, the semi-sensuous engagement of bodies in proximity – likely. You may not set out with eros aforethought, but by the time you've been guided into the room with the glittering lights, picked up the insinuating music, tasted the finger food and sipped at your beverage of choice, your defences will have softened. The feeling doesn't have to be sexual, more a signing up to the flattering social penetration of guest by guest, to the inquisitive exploration of each character's contours. In fact, anything explicitly sexual at a party would make it something else – a theatre of satisfaction rather than of desire, of fruition that has no further fruit in it – whereas the appealingly tensile quality of a good party comes, in part, from the sexual storm remaining unbroken. Even when a party escalates into a saturnalia of other indulgences – drinking, dancing and drugs – sex should remain a private sport, since it pushes against the party's inclusive, egalitarian, democratic inward pull. A party can be the anteroom, but never the bedroom, a touching but not a crossing of the threshold – even the lousy Judy and Johnny, in preference to being caught red-handed, have the decency to slip away.

And although there are many other genres – from children's party to retirement party – it's the kind, like Lesley's, that convenes people in the garden of friendship, while allowing in just a scent of eros to subtly perfume the air, that seems the essence of the party. Even the gathering that assembles long-standing couples who are all friends has, like a Woody Allen movie, the ability to reopen the enquiry that led them to pair off in the first place, to awaken the normally dormant question about each other's attributes as a mate, but not the inclination to pursue it. This is what makes it a party rather than an appointment, a gathering that turns a blind eye to the passing round of an ounce of sexual risk, even if it's tacitly understood no one will partake. For no doubt, in recalculating the amatory worth of individual friends you've long known, the sum will usually work out the same, and yet the party is about the reissuing of your stock *as if* you were touting for love, as a gesture towards the erotic that it's understood won't be further investigated. Why else, in front of old muckers, would you still feel obliged to put on your silks and finery? Long after you've found your mate, the party continues to be a mating ritual, which suggests its real end is not the connubial but nor is it quite a denial of it; you've all agreed to be friends, while recognising that different couples might have formed out of the people in the room and become lovers.

So the modern-day Machiavelli's guide to going to a party might include the following advice. The first rule is that there are no rules: a party can't take off unless you accept a level of uncertainty, unless you arrive with the willingness to be tossed around on its currents that will pitch you into random conversations. Otherwise, it's not a party but an assignment. That said, you don't want to become fortune's fool and end up like Lesley, blindsided by alliances made behind your back. Oscar Wilde declared 'a true friend stabs you in the front' and at the very least you ought to be aware of what's going on – if there's any damage coming your way, try to see it coming. And if that sounds far too cynical, you can take a leaf instead out of Montaigne's book. Rather than establishing a scale of fear, according to which people can find their place in the pecking order, a party, like friendship itself, ought to be the epitome of equable relations among well-intentioned

16

Arguing with your partner

GETTING ANGRY?

Of course not. There's no reason you should – you're just reading a book, which is a pretty peaceful activity. You could even call it passive. After all, you're not doing anything useful, are you? I mean, you're sitting there, not helping particularly – you're hardly making a contribution.

Getting angry now? No? What if I told you I despise you for giving yourself time off to read? For wasting time, when you should be thinking less about yourself and more about others? Does that make you feel good?

OK, maybe you're not rising to the bait. Instead, imagine being on the receiving end of Martha's goading of her husband, George, in the film adaptation of *Who's Afraid of Virginia Woolf?* They've invited a younger, squeaky-clean couple over for dinner at the modest house within the grounds of the university where both men teach. Vulpine and voluptuous Martha, already three sheets to the wind, is bent on provoking the bespectacled, becardiganed George in front of guests who, too polite to intervene, can only become more queasy. In this extract, she's retracing the origins of her marriage's demise:

MARTHA [to the guests]: So anyway, I married the S.O.B. I had it all planned out. First he'd take over the History department – then when Daddy retired, he'd take over the whole college, you know? That was the way it was supposed to be. [to GEORGE] Getting angry, baby, eh? [to the dinner guests] That was the way it was supposed to be. All very simple. And Daddy thought it was a good idea too. For a while. Until he started *watching* for a couple of years. [to GEORGE] Getting angrier? [to the guests] Until he *watched* for a couple of years, and started thinking maybe it wasn't such a good idea after all – that maybe Georgie-boy didn't have the *stuff*, that maybe he didn't have it *in him* –

GEORGE: Stop it, Martha.

MARTHA: Like hell I will! You see, George didn't have much *push*, he wasn't particularly *aggressive*. In fact, he was sort of a flop! A GREAT BIG FAT FLOP!!

[George smashes a bottle of vodka on the mantelpiece]

GEORGE: SHUT UP NOW! Stop it, Martha!

MARTHA: I hope that was an empty bottle, George. You can't afford to waste good liquor! Not on your salary! Not on an ASSOCI-ATE PROFESSOR'S salary!!

George and Martha are played by Richard Burton and Elizabeth Taylor, notorious for the tempestuous nature of their own on and off off-screen relationship, which imparts to Edward Albee's script extra electricity. Nor is its charge all negative – it enriches the erotic complexity, and while George is publicly humiliated, he draws some guilty, private pleasure in being her whipping boy. On this fateful evening, however, Martha takes it too far, her sadism outweighing George's pitiable masochistic yield. In an attempt to punctuate her inexorable onslaught, he breaks the bottle, but it's not enough to bridle her – a fact that only supports her diatribe against a professional feebleness on his part that she so knowingly elides with sexual inadequacy. When Martha scalds that he 'didn't have much *push*, he wasn't particularly *aggressive*. In fact, he was sort of a flop! A GREAT BIG FAT FLOP!!' you don't need to strain to get what she's alluding to, and the empty, broken bottle embodies his shattered manhood. Which would be bad enough, but

Martha enlists two further male figures to show her husband in yet more mocking light. The first is the other man in the room, the tyro set to rocket past the burnt-out satellite that George has been written off as; though quite personable in himself, his very presence, and what it represents, are enough to sharpen the invective that Martha performs before him. The second is the father she calls 'Daddy', as if more proud than ashamed of her infantilised status: this grown woman's wiles include demanding to be treated like a princess and pouring scorn on the financial washout who fails to spoil her. On either side, George finds himself outgunned by a phallus his wife is unabashed in admiring, and he is implicitly confronted with a third: when, later, Martha asserts she 'wears the trousers', she confirms that even she ranks higher than her husband in the pecking order of masculine power.

So why didn't she leave him years ago? Why, if this is the story of spent potency and squandered potential, of a future lost to a historian, didn't she change horses upstream, before her own promise had faded and the alcoholism set in? Well, what George lacks in beef, he makes up for in brains, and in a psychological acumen just as piercing of Martha's own Achilles heel – for she too enjoys being hurt a bit. It's delivered in a different currency – hers gross, his granular, hers scattergun, his surgical – but he gives as good as he gets, which means he and Martha are well matched, even if the match can never be won.

The trouble is that love and war don't go together, even if there's a strand in psychotherapy that recommends argument for surfacing issues and 'working them through' – better to have it out than keep it in. The term comes from the German '*durcharbeiten*', the theory that talking, however painful, can at the very least be palliative, and might just untie the more Gordian knots for good. Except spilling your darkest feelings to a therapist is very different from saying things you might regret to your partner. Where a therapist has no skin in the game, both you and your partner are invested to the gills, neither capable of being objective: rather than providing a salve, the 'talking' between partners risks causing inflammation, the argument serving less to fill in than entrench already dug-in differences.

What's cunning about Martha is that, as if such objectivity were being brought to bear, she elects to wash her dirty laundry in front of other people. By forcing the younger couple to be her witness, she's hoping to make the truth that she sees more widely accepted, making her subjective view more objective. But the witnessing is false: because they are guests, which both enjoins on them decorum and indebts them to their hosts, they are invested in their own way, neutrality unavailable. Clever though Martha's stratagem is, therefore, it's flawed: they aren't going to help her and so, once again, the argument must slog on.

Despite the underhand approach, it's hard not to empathise with her, for Martha models what, when arguing with a partner, many people feel: if only someone else were here to hear this! How could they fail to be on my side?! You long for someone to verify your claims, and when no one appears, you want to cite them in lieu – 'It's not just me who thinks this – your mother said the same thing'; 'If you don't believe me, ask our friends.' In so doing, you're making an appeal to social norms, if not to reason itself – a rhetorical move we'll come back to – but you might also be invoking forces more fundamental. For when men and women argue, there's sometimes an assumption the fault inheres in the man's manness or the woman's womanness – he's taciturn, but she's garrulous; he's obtuse, she's hyper-sensitive – as if each battle were fought between mankind and womankind itself. You can hear this archetypal quality in Martha's ringing accusation of George being too little a man, and George's unspoken reproach that she's too much of a woman – and, because it's archetypal, it's seemingly impossible to resolve. Stalemate again. Man and woman are destined to fight because they are man and woman.

An exit may be found in the French feminism developed in the 70s by Julia Kristeva, Hélène Cixous and Luce Irigaray. All had associations with the journal *Tel Quel*, which coupled left-wing radicalism – even Maoism – with academic abstraction, and cast its contributors as intellectual guerrillas. But if they were feminists, they weren't ones you'd necessarily recognise, because their target wasn't men per se, or even the patriarchal society that favoured men and provoked a parallel resistance across the Atlantic. For while Kristeva and comrades pursued an agenda whose philosophical complexity would always tongue-tie its politics, their American sisters were more direct, burning their bras, marching for equal pay and writing books on how pervasively women's bodies were being exploited. Catalytic though such action might have been for the cause, however, it only reinforced the false assumption that, to the French writers, had caused the battle of the sexes in the first place. Known as 'essentialism', this was the idea of an essential maleness or femaleness, and against it all three writers united. By fighting for women, you're defending woman, or protecting an ideal essence on her behalf, of which there's no real proof. Even today you can't deny that men and women get treated differently at work, say, and it's as beyond doubt as ever that biological characteristics set them apart, but jumping from such empirical observations about the sexes to an essence of man, as distinct from an essence of woman, is, from the French feminist perspective, to leap too far. Difference of genitalia doesn't equate to difference of essence, and testosterone and oestrogen are merely physical, not metaphysical, substances. So, if an essential maleness or femaleness exists – and there's the rub – it would have to go deeper than the body. Both essential femaleness and essential maleness would have to be divorced from biological gender – a bizarre enough thought, yet in their own role-reversing antics, even George and Martha prove the point: George irks Martha for his womanness, Martha irks George for her manness, and in both cases the behaviour has cut loose from the biology. They argue because each believes the other has compromised the essence of their gender. They argue, in other words, *in the name of* an essential maleness and femaleness – which, for the French feminists, is precisely the problem. All essentialism carries the risk of violence, because once you stick up for an ideal essence, be it woman, liberty or America, it will lead you into conflict with those whose ideal essences don't conform. So when you argue with your partner (and we're assuming a heterosexual relationship), you might, without realising, be claiming they've fallen short of the essential maleness or femaleness you were harbouring in your head. The lesson being that if this private, divisive essentialism is something you can let go of, the two of you might live more peaceably.

Assuming peace is your goal. The trouble with arguments is they acquire a life of their own, in which being right can overtake finding resolution. At its height – or depth – a thrashing argument features two certainties that won't be reconciled, each party adamant they're in the right and convinced of the erroneousness of the other's so-called truth. Given such a stand-off, you'll more than likely appeal to reason, a force to transcend the argument and take it into the incontestable sphere of eternal verity – where, amazingly enough, the overarching truth you've evoked backs you up. Or – what amounts to the same thing – you'll pick apart your partner's reasoning as illogical, as failing the requirements of 'common sense' – for which read 'personal preference'. Either way, the rationality you invoke may be but a veil for your emotions, a sly or even self-deceiving attempt to dress up your seething and subjective feelings as incontestable. And apart from all the psychological game-playing that implies, such tricks reveal the main resource of argument as rhetoric – an argument being a series of verbal feints designed to manoeuvre your interlocutor into submission.

Not that rhetoric and psychology don't go together: when Martha asks George, twice, if he's getting angry, it's by pulling both levers at once that she yanks his chain. A literally rhetorical question – 'Getting angry, baby?' – it is posed without expectation of a reply, a statement disguised as an enquiry; at the same time, she's ascribing to her husband an emotional state (anger) that the question itself, being rhetorical, helps generate. It's this formula of rhetoric + psychology that gives Martha the edge, and is probably the formula for all argument. For arguing is indeed formulaic, so much so that the ancient Greeks and Romans, who developed the art of rhetoric, catalogued every last linguistic trick – including the rhetorical question itself, which they called '*erotema*' – that you might deploy. In so doing, they were aiming well beyond mere scholarly satisfaction, towards equipping politicians with the tools of persuasion they'd need to build support for their policies – you're far less likely to get someone to vote for you if you can't persuade them of your merits, and that takes language.

Nor have those techniques become outdated – take only the first eight words of the inaugural address spoken by Barack Obama: 'My fellow citizens, I stand here today humbled.'

'My fellow citizens' is an *apostrophe*, a formal address to an audience, whose distance has been shortened by the insertion of the *ad hominem* term 'fellow' – that is, an ingratiating suggestion to his audience that they start out on his side. The word 'citizens', neutral enough, is actually a *euphemism*, or understatement, for Obama has revised the *apostrophe* made famous by George W. Bush, 'My fellow Americans', so that 'citizens' stands for 'not just Americans' – that is, we're no longer isolationists, but citizens of a world we share with others. 'I stand here today humbled' works on *antithesis*, a putting of terms into opposition with each other, whereby 'stand', apart from connoting the witness stand and stealing some of its sincerity, erects an uprightness to contrast with the lowness of 'humbled', from the Latin *'humus'*, meaning 'earth'; and this also loops back to the word 'fellow', to suggest fellow creatures who inhabit the earth: we are all creatures but also citizens, equally low but all high, just as the President is also one of the people. The preceding word, 'today', is a *metonym*, a singularity alluding to a more general phenomenon – Obama doesn't just mean today, Tuesday 20 January 2009, but 'the times we live in', with a tacit reference to the crisis he finds himself inheriting; this is also an *ad populum* device, a playing on the audience's emotions, for before any logical case is made, Obama touches on the fearful emotions Americans might be feeling at that juncture. And that's just the first eight words.

If such ancient devices thrive in modern politics, so the arguments you have with your partner may be parsed or broken down in the same way. Imagine the following dialogue:

SHE: You don't love me any more.
HE: Are you crazy?
SHE: You never say anything nice.

HE: I asked you to marry me six months ago! I'm not exactly uncommitted.

SHE: It doesn't feel like that ... It feels like you're using me somehow.

HE: And you're so attuned to feelings, right?

SHE: What's that supposed to mean?

And now consider the psycho-rhetorical tricks in use:

SHE: You don't love me any more. [insinuation: stating a hypothesis to test its veracity]

HE: Are you crazy? [appeal to reason: I'm sane, you're mad]

SHE: You never say anything nice. [*hyperbole* or exaggeration]

HE: I asked you to marry me six months ago! [appeal to facts, even though they may not be the whole truth] I'm not exactly uncommitted. [*litotes*: use of the double negative to add ironic force to a statement]

SHE: It doesn't feel like that [*ad hominem* use of subjective data for lack of objective fact] ... It feels like you're using me somehow. [the non-specificity of 'somehow' renders it too nebulous to defend against, making it an argument by mystery]

HE: And you're so attuned to feelings, right? [*erotema*, now with the force of sarcastic imputation]

SHE: What's that supposed to mean? [a more sophisticated form of *erotema*, whereby the petitioner defies the respondent to provide an answer, and where silence would represent the petitioner's victory]

They might not think they're being 'rhetorical' at all, but each partner will draw from an arsenal of rhetorical weapons. Which suggests a rhetoric-free language might not exist, with some modern critics going so far as to say the rhetoric determines what you want to say, rather than the other way round: before you've begun to speak, the suite of rhetorical devices available will shape your intentions, and once you start, it will steer you like computer chess through one of a number of pre-wired permutations.

Despite their indefatigability in itemising the rhetorical moves, the ancients stopped short of so anti-humanist a line. And they did so to protect their concept of truth, which depended on rhetoric as a foil, something for the truth to contrast with, the better to stand out. For rhetoric can go to your head, bamboozling you with all its linguistic gizmos and leading you to argue for this cause or that just because you can. Like a thoroughbred horse that's bucked its rider, rhetoric can, without the truth to steer it, continue to gallop handsomely but in completely the wrong direction. However, it's precisely this failing on the part of rhetoric which provides your best comeback against it. Say your partner is the more skilled arguer and you leave each quarrel with a disquieting sense of having been wrong-footed: at least you can charge him or her with twisting your words and using cunning tricks to distort the facts. The slicker the rhetoric, the more questionable the truth, and the less morally sound the orator. It's all in the opening of *King Lear*, where the two ugly sisters use their silver tongues to garner their father's gold, and where Cordelia, the youngest, proves her sincerity through the paucity and guilelessness of her language, her linguistic poverty signifying moral wealth. Being short of words doesn't stop you owning the moral high ground.

Now set language aside and ask yourself what it is, at bottom, that makes you and your partner argue. There'll be some things you'll identify quickly – conflicting values, misaligned expectations, poor communication. But what if the drive to argue went deeper still?

Towards the finale of *Who's Afraid of Virginia Woolf?*, George and Martha make a pact of 'total war', but because it's agreed with gusto – because it's a *pact* – we, the viewer, are encouraged to see how barely their hate differs from their love: after all, as psychoanalysis points out, both feelings involve a deep preoccupation with another person, a paying them intense psychic attention. When going into battle with a partner, our war instincts might not be so easy to disentangle from sentiments of love, and what buzzes during an argument is the tension between pushing the partner away and pulling them close. In the theory of war devised by the right-wing thinker of the Nazi era

feel sexual – in the same way you decide to make a sandwich or take a walk – you reply to something activated in you. Regardless of one person having 'initiated' it, sex is never about leading, always about following – and before initiating, even the initiator will have been beckoned towards its suggestive shrine. Sure, it can be scheduled – you could arrange to meet a lover at a motel at three in the afternoon and the erotic thrill might be the greater – but the success of the assignation will depend on a third element. If, having checked in, you're not going to perch awkwardly on the crisp sheets, at least one of you will have to allow this 'urge' to become urgent. The urge must be received, the call answered. All of which suggests the phrase 'having sex' gets the order wrong – sex has us.

So, if not directly from you, whence does this 'drive' for sex come? Does it whoosh about in the air, flapping blindly like Cupid, pinging an arrow your way at random to prick your lust? Is it down to the rhythm of chemicals in your system? An explanation of a kind comes in Plato's *Symposium* – the transcript of a party where the game is to come up with theories of love – voiced by one of the guests, the comic playwright, Aristophanes. He relates the myth that originally 'each human being was a rounded whole, with double back and flanks forming a complete circle; it had four hands and an equal number of legs, and two identically similar faces upon a circular neck, with one head common to both faces, which were turned in opposite directions'. But the combined force of these early humans, and the hubris that went with it, so alarmed the gods that Zeus had them all chopped in half, with the broken skin tied in the middle with a knot that formed the belly button. Ever since, the severed individuals have been seeking to come back to their other half, defining sex – the gluing of fragments – as the deep satisfaction of being once more complete. Aristophanes's story holds no biological water, of course, but like many myths it makes up for it in psychological insight: it interprets the craving for sex as nostalgia, a desire for return to a lost paradise of wholeness and haleness, a site of familiarity and sameness. In tumbling into the exquisite comfort of a lover's arms, you are seeking to repair your perforated soul.

Hmm. Sounds lovely, but it's corrupted by the implication that having sex means sleeping with yourself. OK, it mightn't have quite the unwholesomeness of masturbation, but this having sex with what is literally your other half suggests that, to enable you to see yourself reflected back, your lust becomes the burning away of any face a lover might present, a peeling back of their personal properties to disclose your own, and that's no less graceless. As the compulsion to refind yourself, the urge for sex views any lover's intrinsic qualities as a barrier: you're not after that person, except in so far as they offer a conduit back to you. In this interpretation, it's not difference but sameness that causes arousal.

Aristophanes's fanciful answer on the origin of sex describes a backward-looking, even atavistic enterprise – you have sex to get back to where you once belonged – but if the question is 'Where does the sex drive come from?' a theory easier on modern ears lies in evolutionary psychology, which shifts the emphasis from past to future: the reason for having sex is furthering the species. It fails to account for the sex you have just for fun – using contraceptives, say – let alone same-sex encounters, but it helps explain the urgency of the urge. That melting in the loins, the darting enquiry from the midst of your body that seeks from your partner a corresponding reaction, the promissory arc that binds you together – all are ruses on the part of the species in its mission to splice you together with another being.

And without them, consider, what would happen? What if sex were tiresome or painful? The species would die out. A life force it may be, but at this species level sex is life as the resistance to death, the persistent effort to persist. Where, in Aristophanes's legend, sex brings closure or completion, now it gestures ahead to newness, with the consummation between two lovers the joining of two semicircles for life to pass through; in so doing, the lovers are implicated in their own death, for if they were deathless or immortal, there'd be no need to create new life. To be about furthering the species, sex has to involve the dying out of the present generation – as the next wave furls up behind, its energy rearing, the first wave crashes.

By this account, sexual pleasure becomes what Theodor Adorno, founder of the mid-twentieth-century Frankfurt School of social theory, condemned as a biological trick to preserve the species – like a sinister ideology that gets you to do what it wants, it tosses you a sop to stop you asking difficult questions. Sexual pleasure might feel highly localised on you, your partner and the erogenous tie between you both, but it's merely the mist sprayed over you and others by the species' drone as it cultivates the millions of its crops. If it tingles, well, good for you. Caused by absorbing the fertilizing chemicals, the kick in your heart rate during arousal is as much a first salvo from the life aspiring to be bred from you as the pounding of your own adrenalin. What you're feeling isn't unreal, but, in anticipation of your being survived, the pleasure, the pleasingness, has your death shuddering inside it – small wonder that orgasm has so often been likened to decease, and gets referred to as the '*petit mort*' or 'little death'. And that's tragic, to Adorno's mind, not because during sex we traverse death's shadow, but because it makes us androids, executing a plan for the sake of a collective whose only goal is to reproduce the collective.

What's worse, the argument about preserving the species threatens to break the link, so often desired by modern lovers, between sex and love. Neither the Darwinistic narrative of sex for survival nor, for that matter, Aristophanes's fable of the self's homecoming thinks of sex needing love to make it work, and that's perhaps why both, as theories, feel unsatisfying. The Greeks had a myth about us being cleft in two by the immortals? Fine – it's a nice story. There's an evolutionary impulse in having sex? So what – it doesn't give sex a meaning, it just furnishes it with a function. For us today, the special thing about sex is the combining of erotic pleasure with loving-kindness, the physical with the emotional. It's what distinguishes human from animal coitus, and it takes the edge off the brutishness an onlooker might mistake it for. In sex, the meshing of bodies, while not above delivering animal satisfaction, serves as an analogy for the higher interfusion of minds that goes on in parallel. But they're not coextensive: in this modern conception of sex, the love arrives before and dwells long after the rubbing and the rutting, so if lust is the trigger of sex, then love triggers the trigger.

According to biblical tradition love can, in turn, be subdivided into friendship ('philia') and spiritual or emotional love ('agape'), which complicates the relationship with sex – or 'eros' – a bit further. What about sex with friends, for example? If a friend is someone you like but don't love, is it OK to sleep with them? There's sexual attraction (eros) and there's friendship (philia), but there's no agape. So is two out of three enough? Of course, if you're in a relationship with someone else you *do* love, friend-sex definitely isn't acceptable, but what if you sleep with a friend while you're both single? Does the fact that there's none of that spiritual or emotional love – none of that agape – mean the sex is morally wrong? Must eros always be leavened with love to stop it from being merely sexual and therefore somewhat dirty? That biblical tradition would say yes. In fact, in its Roman Catholic version, it would prefer you didn't have sex at all, but if you must, then it's best to do it with love, within marriage and for the purposes of procreation. But even if you do temper sex with love, certain things must come to pass for sex to have occurred, things which are not ostensibly to do with love at all, hence the difference between them: not orgasm or even penetration, necessarily, but without the mutual stimulation of erogenous functions – even by phone, email or webcam – sex is just a decorous exchange. However much love or friendship contributes to it, sex has, in order to be sex, to pass above, or beneath, those more elevated states: there has to be some action.

Perhaps this explains the long tradition concerning sexual technique: if love and friendship had everything in the sack sewn up, there'd be no need for all those manuals on the positions; and because it's fundamentally different, sex looks for a different language, and finds it in the grammars of fucking. From the *Kama Sutra* to *The Joy of Sex* and beyond, sex has lent itself to being codified in instruction leaflets not unrelated to flat-pack guidelines: there's a right and a wrong way to connect the parts, one leading to satisfaction, the other to frustration and toil – where the 2D picture refuses to be coaxed into 3D reality and too many screws are left over. In these primers, it's clear there's a skill to 'lovemaking', as it's euphemistically called, just as there's a skill to t'ai chi or lithography, which means that although having sex might be the most natural thing in the world, it shouldn't be approached as such: it probably took some artifice to get as far as the bedroom, so why, at the last minute, rush it? Take Ovid's *Ars Amatoria*, which, though written at about the time of Christ's virgin birth, gives the would-be lover step-by-step hints not just on what to do in bed, but on how to get a girl into it – his first piece of advice being to tell her that you love her, whether it's true or not. So prized is the end result, it can't be left to chance, and the steps leading up to it must be practised with diligence. And once in bed, the manuals aren't just anatomical, they're dynamic – studies in stress mechanics, enquiries into the forces most likely to produce intensity. Thus, when explaining bondage, *The Joy of Sex* analyses 'the critical areas where compression boosts sex', these being the 'wrists, ankles, elbows (don't try to make them meet by brute force), soles of the feet, thumbs and big toes'. The sexual body is construed as an instrument of infinite variety, to be tuned or detuned according to the finesse you bring to it.

That artistry declares itself in Alex Comfort's subtitle, *A Gourmet Guide to Lovemaking*. While the phrase 'having sex' suggests nothing more than a transaction, to qualify as a sexual gourmet involves sampling exotic flavours and transforming your bland diet into a smorgasbord of delicacies to be grazed on at whim. The book itself breaks down into 'starters', 'main courses', 'sauces and pickles', and it's these latter condiments of dangerous relish that are crucial, the side dishes central, because they make sex the art it should be, a declining of meat and potatoes for a taste of the unusual – a broaching of the inner temple hitherto reserved for princes and their geishas. It's always about parting the veil and then tiptoeing a little further to a more delicious place – delicious *because* forbidden, a transport beyond where you began, your bed a magic carpet that takes you to unimagined lands.

It's this emphasis on secret knowledge that, ironically perhaps, connects the art of sex with the religious experience from which it borrows much of its language – the two converging especially on the idea of ecstasy. Consider this, from the Spanish mystic of the sixteenth century, St Teresa of Avila:

> The pain was so great, that it made me moan; and yet so surpassing was the sweetness of this excessive pain, that I could not wish to be rid of it … It is a caressing of love so sweet which now takes place between the soul and God, that I pray God of His goodness to make him experience it who may think that I am lying.

The modern, psychologically savvy sceptic might find little of surprise in a nun channelling her suppressed sexual energy into theological rapture, but the link is more subtle than it seems. If the membrane separating religious from sexual ecstasy is so very fine, it's because both nestle within a larger organ of emotion that presses them together. That emotion is one of self-undoing. In both the ecstatic swooning of sexual crescendo and the epiphanic surrounding of divine light, the lover's self first submits, then dissolves – again, it's about being had, rather than having – into a thousand pleasure particles, the body momentarily transformed into a soul. A cloud of unknowing descends, the faculties of cognition and identity immobilised, and for this achingly long-short bitter-sweet period you experience a dissolution that may well be the nearest on earth you'll ever get to heaven. Again, you are carried across a threshold unperceived by the masses – and that's the point of making sex a matter of carefully constructed design: it unlocks the recesses the multitude are otherwise denied.

You don't have to buy the connection between sex and religion, of course, but if you think that trying to turn your lovemaking into an art is spurious or silly, you'd better be sure your partner feels the same – it's not unlikely they will make their own assessment of your performance, willy-nilly. Yet for many couples, such candid conversations about sexual proficiency lie out of bounds, because that would be to concede sex can indeed be separated from love, divorced from the relationship, and once that happens, it doesn't automatically become a matter of artfulness – it can equally turn into porn. In other words, once love gets taken out of the equation, the sex left over can be interpreted in more than one way: if, on the one hand, it's a high-walled sanctuary where experts refine their skills in private, on the other it's an exposed, brightly lit arena for the naked pursuit of genital stimulation. Which must be why, for all their poise, the instruction manuals never quite lift away from the top-shelf magazines they want to look down on. A leaf through *The Joy of Sex*, with its tasteful charcoals of sensual exploration between two emotionally mature, liberal-minded adults, might be educational in a pseudo-scientific sort of way, but it can't be sure to stop its reader's libidinal sap rising and brimming over the dry taxonomy of coital permutations.

Again, you might not welcome pornography getting this close to your otherwise healthy sex life. Even if, to help things along, you draw on X-rated material, you might be offended by the claim that the love you go on to make itself involves anything pornographic. But what if some of your pleasure comes from looking at your partner, or at yourself with your partner? Or what if the lights are off but, as your body shivers, tantalised, beneath your lover's touch, your mind fills with lewd imagery? There's a school of thought going back to French philosopher Georges Bataille – a contemporary of Theodor Adorno – which argues that, once the eye is involved, mind's eye included, obscenity has begun. Whereas that delectable touching has to be done up close and personal (you can't touch someone more than an arm's length away, and caressing a photograph doesn't count), looking can be done from a distance – where distance invites the looker to appraise, objectify and control what it looks at. Looking breaks free from the intimate bonds of touching and opens into a dimension ungoverned by tactile trust, where anything goes and where, therefore, you can demand what you actually see to replicate what you see, uncensored, in your head.

To this theme of uninhibited looking Bataille devotes *Story of the Eye*, a 'novel' so extreme that, for the further arousal of its adolescent lovers, already mesmerised by each other's ever filthier performances, an eyeball itself becomes a fetish object – if there's a gourmet aspect to sex, then for Bataille the eye replaces the mouth as the chief erotic organ. But the main point is that the extremism of the subject matter is matched by the language. It's not so much that the book abounds in four-letter words – though it has its fair share – nor that it tries to be as theatrical in its phrasing as the sexual stunts it describes, but that, on the contrary, it describes them with such utter frankness and detachment. That's why I put 'novel' in quotation marks: it feels less like the work of imagination than reportage; it reads like dispatches from a war correspondent. Nothing escapes its implacable stare and there's no shade to shelter in.

The irony is that, because the vile bodies and their actions are so graphically narrated, Bataille's book fails the first test of pornography, which is to titillate – and in this it might inadvertently be proving a point made by one of his philosophical counterparts, Michel Foucault (whom we discovered earlier, at the gym, talking about exercise as a form of state control). On the subject of sex, Bataille's text might seem as far from being repressed as it's possible to get, but in his *History of Sexuality* Foucault hints at a pitfall in such explicit material. Because sex has become so central a part of everyday discourse, we might think we're less repressed than the Victorians, but what's actually happened is that the discourse itself becomes a form of repression – that is, instead of having more sex, we talk more about it, and so delude ourselves that we're more liberated. And after all, there's something about *Story of the Eye* which is more likely to produce analysis – like this very essay – than tempt us into the bedroom.

Falling asleep and dreaming

TIME FOR BED. You've had quite a day – fending off the savage
hordes on the way to work, running for your life at the gym, keeping
your friends from plotting against you – and you can look forward
to some well-earned rest. Tomorrow you'll fight another day, but for
now, as night draws in, blessed slumber is yours. Unless you're an
insomniac, tormented by the demi-devils who swarm into your mind
and prick it with tiny pitchforks of worry, you are, for a few treasured
hours, being let off the hook.

And this going off duty is so important, because it suggests that,
apart from restoration, the main function of sleep is to treat us with
compassion, and it's captured in W. H. Auden's 'Lullaby':

> Lay your sleeping head, my love,
> Human on my faithless arm;
> Time and fevers burn away
> Individual beauty from
> Thoughtful children, and the grave
> Proves the child ephemeral:
> But in my arms till break of day
> Let the living creature lie,
> Mortal, guilty, but to me
> The entirely beautiful.

As you fall asleep – and the idea of falling matters, because it's about surrendering control and responsibility – your humanity rises, since there's nothing, while sleeping, you can do to stand out, no action you'll be taking, by definition, to demarcate you from others or testify to your specialness. Though polarised in the cut and thrust of daylight, prince and pauper, saint and sinner, all, as unconscious bodies, are smoothed out by the hand of sleep; literally a levelling experience, the state of lying asleep displays each resting head as equal, no matter what heroism – or villainy – it perpetrated that day. The 'sleeping head' is only 'human'.

It's almost impossible to judge or condemn the sleeping face – you'd need even the wickedest criminal to wake up before you could really start to feel scorn – for the sleeping face presents an innocence that has nothing to do with morality. Partly it's the sheer defencelessness of those who are asleep, of course, but if it's not *moral* innocence you read on the closed eyelids and slowly beating pulse of the neck of those who sleep, it's the innocence of being unclaimed, of not being associated with this or that, of holding back from belonging. You have to wait until they get up to know where they stand and so, during sleep's intermission, you can only suspend judgement. By the standards of daylight, the sleeping head in the poem may well be 'guilty', but when Auden asks us to 'Let the living creature lie', it's so as not to disturb this fragile hiatus. The state of amoral innocence is precious, and we should let it be. There'll be plenty of time tomorrow for accusations.

Not the least reason for suspending judgement of the sleeping head is that it's already sentenced to being 'mortal', a fact proved by our need to sleep at all. No, we are not superhuman, unlike immortal deities, for whom the very fact that they're immortal means their energy knows no limit and they've no need to recharge themselves. Conversely, therefore, for us, it's because we die that we need to sleep. You might think that sleeping would give us more energy to keep going longer, but no – the fact that we need to sleep at all means our energy is finite – because our life is finite too. By referring to the 'grave', Auden shows how the bed prefigures the big sleep to come; the tiredness 'proves the child ephemeral', for even the young, with their whole life ahead, have their expiration built in. Fatigue, fallibility and finitude – three human conditions sleep exists to recognise.

And yet beneath the peacefulness on the face of those who sleep – a state that elicits a compassionate calm of your own – are fireworks to outglow most things in waking life. The body may be at rest, but the mind, far from taking a break, goes into overdrive, inventing fantasies like there's no tomorrow; so rich and remarkable are the dreams you dream, it's as if every other system in your body that might use up energy had to be shut down. In this sense, sleep is a great deceiver – it might look like innocence, but who knows what guilty secrets are showing in the cinema of the mind. The strange thing is, the dreamer is deceived too.

To crack the code, we must turn to Freud, whose *Interpretation of Dreams* marked, at the turn of the nineteen century and into the twentieth, a bridge from naïvety to knowledge, since when it's become much less easy to write dreams off as innocuous froth or bizarre fancy. Of course, there had been theories of dreams for centuries before, and Freud's masterwork opens with a survey of what he considers the pre-scientific era – before, that is, the psychoanalytic academy he founded brought to dream analysis due rigour and method. Broadly, this was a period of superstition, which took dreams to be the visitations by forces either demonic or divine, keen to transmit messages to their terrestrial kin. Which might explain the dream's prophetic quality: if it provides you with a premonition, it's not that overnight you've acquired the psychic powers of a shaman; rather, your mind was turned into a deposit box for the use of prescient spirits who left in it riddling warnings about the shape of things to come.

From that benighted tradition, Freud nevertheless preserves two concepts. The first is the dream as missive. Of course, it would be odd to think dreams entirely devoid of message and therefore meaning – how would you explain them otherwise? Perhaps if every single night you dreamed the identical dream, you might write it off as, for example, a bodily reflex caused by the dwindling during sleep of the metabolic rate; but because the variation from dream to dream is so huge, because each night the theatre puts on a new show – one time you're a baboon climbing over a photocopier, another your mother has dyed her hair green – it's almost perverse not to infer from that variety some significance. Why differ if not to carry different portents? Accordingly, Freud continues to believe the dream a message, but rather than assuming its meaning was sent down from a mysterious cloud, he says it gurgles up from within, making it a message to oneself. True, that mysterious cloud might itself produce a variety of dreams, and therefore be seen to be generating 'meaning', but because Freud wants to present himself as an enlightened scientist, he won't be doing with such arcana. And in effect, that's the first step towards making dream study scientific: the dream is located in a sphere – the brain – that, unlike the realm of the spirits, is knowable; by having its provenance located in the person that hosts it, the dream may submit more usefully to the scrutiny of the scientist, especially the scientist equipped with the implements, the trowels and tape measures, for mental archaeology.

So Freud is saying that when you dream, it is indeed *you* that's dreaming, rather than some external agency rolling out your psyche as a screen for its own communications. Wish or whimsy, sex or sadism, fright or flight, the stuff of dreams redounds to you, with no one else to point the finger at – you can't plead innocence of your dreams, not without reverting to the theory of being visited by spirits which Freud was so keen to overcome. Put that together with Freud's second borrowing from the ancient tradition, that dreams are secrets, and the mixture explodes. These most inner images, the ones that come to you in the privacy of sleep, in the unguardedness of lying down and from your psychic midst – this phantomic caravan of images generated by you and you alone aren't just bizarre to those you might report them to, they're unintelligible *even to you*, their author. Fine, the ancients might have considered dreams enigmatic, but being the works of shadowy spirits, angels or demons, what else would you expect? If such spirits *didn't* communicate in runes, they'd be less than supernatural and you'd be disappointed; but to think you might speak to *yourself* with similar equivocation, that you might send yourself messages to defeat your own interpretation of them, takes the power of dream to another level. The fact that we dream means, in the words of Nietzsche, 'we are strangers to ourselves'.

How is that possible? To square the circle, Freud proposes possibly the most important concept of the modern era – the unconscious. Inside us, while sleeping, there's a communications agency devising messages of a complexity that leaves us, on waking, as perplexed as the audience at a piece of experimental theatre – where the audience is also the playwright, cast and director. The unconscious, which belongs to us but exceeds our control, is at work. And if the play is so confusing, it's because the material has been censored – twice, in fact – and we're barred from seeing the original. For 'censoring' doesn't mean 'deleting' so much as altering, and the first censoring process probably happened in childhood, when your psyche developed along the following lines.

As a baby, you were all about wanting – mainly you wanted oral gratification – and had concern for little else. All that mattered was me, me, me – a phenomenon Freud baptised as *'Das Ich'* or the I (this usually gets translated as 'ego', but it was, and is, odd to translate German into Latin for an English audience). You were a wanting I, and for the most part, you got what you wanted – your mama fed you, your mouth was full. Before long, however, you sense in your father or sibling something less beneficent than love – they too want a stake in the mother, and you become aware of treacherous competition. Your access to the mother's breast, suddenly, seems regulated and the epoch of uninterrupted gratification over. Desires formerly indulged meet with constraint or deferral, and you have no choice but to repress them – at which point they start forming the stagnant build-up known as your unconscious. You've learned your first lesson – you can't always get what you want – and the thwarting energy makes in your mind a vector that conducts frustrated wishes towards an underground depository to lie dormant. It's from this unhealthful pond of drowned wishes that your dream material will later be dredged.

This is the first level of censorship – by the time the dream show lights up the inner walls of your brain, it will have already, as the repressed matter from your infancy, spent years submerged in your psyche. Not all that material will have taken the form of yearnings for your mother's body, or for oral satisfaction, but its general character will be of wishes impeded, hopes frustrated, desires checked – material, in all cases, you held back from public expression. This fact alone goes some way in explaining a dream's weirdness, for what you're seeing is a parade of what to your psyche is ancient history, a sequence of images wrested from a pile put aside in childhood, come back to haunt and taunt you.

So how is it that our dreams often feature material from much later in our lives, even the day of the dream itself? It's not like every dream is set in the home you grew up in, or stars your folks as young parents. Well, this is where the second censoring comes in – the dream takes old experiences and disguises them in new clothes. A simple example: you dream about arguing with your boss, but he's a stand-in for your father, and the argument re-enacts a childhood scene when you wanted to play in the garden but weren't allowed. The dream uses recent material to dress up and smuggle in the unfinished business from your youth. And why would it do that? Why not just dream about the original argument? Remember, your psyche's reason for repressing the primary material was that it represented a wish (you wanted to play in the garden) that you were prevented from fulfilling, and so buried; but had you simply stowed it with all that boiling emotion, it might have scorched your mind. Part of repression's job is to draw some of the heat, to take the sting out of the tail, and it does that by smudging the picture of the upsetting event before it gets locked in your mental safe – a repressed memory isn't the same as an ordinary memory, which can be held comfortably near the front of your mind; it's far more brash and violent, and needs to be doped up and dispatched to your head's high-security wing. In this sense, it's impossible to remember a traumatic event with accuracy, because, to whatever degree, it will have been reprogrammed, disfigured, lobotomised in transit to the unconscious's archive. This would explain the notorious unreliability of eyewitness accounts – if you've been party to something terrifying, then to spare you from its resurgence, your mind instinctively will distort it before transferring it into your memory. Occasionally, however, as in Post-Traumatic Stress Disorder, the initial incident held such horror, there was no taming it before it got locked away, and it comes back again and again in full force, yanking its victims over to the point in psychic time when the dreadful event took place.

In sum, your dreams represent the distorted memories of unrequited wishes from long ago. The original material will never be recovered – you're dreaming about it only because you repressed it, and in the act of repression, like a master forger doctoring documents, you corrupted it – but it continues to set off your dreams. Hence the two levels of censorship that interpose themselves before the dream is dreamed – the choking back of the wish itself when it couldn't be realised, and the editing you did on it before accepting into your unconscious the trauma it would otherwise represent. And on top of those 'censoring' mechanisms, there are two more. Freud says the dream material isn't only altered, it's abridged. In our simple example, the boss might represent, in addition to your father, yourself – you, your own worst enemy, perhaps, disguised as your boss, are in argument with yourself. The boss becomes not just a father substitute, but the representative of a personal failing – the dream's ability for efficient condensation means a single figure might contain multiple personae. Lastly, *in the very act of dreaming*, you'll be making the further edits that Freud terms 'secondary revision'. Unconscious yes, but guileless no, dreaming is an activity during which the sleeping mind is far from asleep, its guard not quite lowered against the upsurge of material that, if allowed into the light, it might yet consider inappropriate.

No wonder Freud called his book *The Interpretation of Dreams*: if they are built up from so many panes of refraction that sit on top of each other, if they put so much effort into throwing us off the scent, then dreams cry out for some analysis, some unpeeling of the onion, even in the knowledge that what awaits us at the core is nothing. Or do they? If they're never going to reveal their inner meaning, why bother? Freud would argue that interpreting your dreams reduces anxiety: it helps you understand the unconscious blockages interfering with your waking life – analysing your boss dream, for example, might lead you, on waking, to reflect that you're not seeing the man for who he is, but projecting on to him feelings that belong with your father, or you, or both. In being disabused of theories you hold about difficult people in your life, you might spare yourself a good degree of worry; it blows away the cobwebs in your mind, freeing you to look at people afresh.

You can see why psychoanalysis – a conversation between analyst and patient that's typically conducted for fifty minutes a day, five days a week and for upwards of five years – becomes such a drawn-out process. Sifting through just one dream's disparate evidence is a painstaking business, and because it's highly specific to you and your pathology, only so many general rules can be applied. But if the Freudian dream is such a bespoke artefact, his erstwhile colleague – and subsequent rival – Carl Jung developed a theory in which your dreams would fit into a far narrower range of categories. He found the notion of a personal unconscious not invalid, but inadequate, and supplemented it with a 'collective unconscious' from which, among other things, the imagery of dreams would arise. Although the Freudian dream happily plunders material from your childhood, it can't avail itself of anything before birth, whereas its Jungian counterpart will exploit the image reserves from the dawn of mankind – for the collective unconscious works like folk memory, a subliminal passing down through the generations of icons whose origin will never be recovered, which therefore confers on them a mysteriousness. While such images flit from mind to mind on a nocturnal telepathic circuit, their persistence over time – over centuries – builds an independence that Jungians sometimes consider to betray the presence of an *anima mundi*, or 'world-soul'. The collective unconscious, in other words, adds up to more than the aggregate of personal unconsciouses, becoming a property of the world itself, and when you dream at night, it's the world-soul dreaming through you.

That lends each dream image an archaic, indeed archetypical, character, so despite broadening the personal unconscious to encompass all humanity, the collective version contains fewer rather than more images – limited, like Tarot cards, with their Fool, Magician, High Priestess and so on to a select pantheon of stock figures considered to be eternal. Among the most compelling must be the Shadow. While each of us has a Self – the form of our identity and an archetype in its own right, because so universal – that Self surprisingly does not contain everything true about us, and in dreams, our less complimentary facets, embodied by the Shadow, may appear. In the argument with your boss, for example, the Self would be represented by you and your Shadow by him, where he manifests that side of you you'd rather disavow. You consider yourself a reflective, conciliatory type, known for your empathy, quite the opposite of the bully you report to at work – but that bully is part of you. Which doesn't make you a Jekyll and Hyde, for if every Self has a Shadow, the interloper serves not to dilute but to concentrate who you are. Your Shadow is exactly that – the darkness thrown off by your light that remains largely inactive, and it draws off the blacker aspects of your spirit for the brighter parts to shine.

Whether you're in bed with Freud or Jung, night-time brings not calm but commotion in our mental activity, as if an infrared camera were switched on in the jungle to film the previously unseen wild shenanigans. There's even the possibility that daytime is the rest from night – after all, in their thrilling dramatics, our dreams make the routines we go through at work look awfully dull; not to mention the fact that we'll spend about twenty years of our lives asleep, so it's hardly a marginal activity. But what about the period at night when you're not dreaming, there's no REM, nor flicker of any kind? Investigating it at all causes problems, because no one can report back on what happened – it's a place you go to every night, but is no more retrievable than dark matter. As I said in the first chapter, when exploring waking up, if you're not dreaming, and there's no mental activity to speak of, there's a case for saying that the depths of night really are a kind of inexistence. Not that this need be a frightening fact; on the contrary, if you're someone who's afraid of dying, for example, you can console yourself that every night you will have experienced a version of death – or, rather, you didn't 'experience' it at all, because you weren't conscious enough to be experiencing anything – and it wasn't so bad.

The closest we can get to any representation of this dark time, perhaps, would be sleepwalking. For, as unremembered activity, sleepwalking is actually less enigmatic than the unremembered inactivity of deep sleep – or the often remembered inactivity of dreaming. And yet it is still mysterious, so what of this zombie-like state? The word *sleepwalking* does well to be an oxymoron, a combining of two incompatibles, for to walk while you sleep is to go against nature. At least, that is the orthodox view, and witnesses have described the eerie robotics that cause the sleepwalker to get out of bed, open the window and, in the most fatal cases, jump. The actions of the sleepwalker appear cognitively enabled, but the faculty of judgement has been numbed, and the whole procedure gives off a mechanical air that resembles toys coming to life at night.

The less orthodox stance, taken by recent theorists of cyber culture, argues that such automatism represents less an aberration than the general condition of a 'post-human' age. In this account, sleepwalking merely illustrates how we are all possessed – even constituted – by the machine. We're not only surrounded by mechanical devices, we've started to behave like them, while our 'humanity', in proportion, grows weak. We reproduce ideas without thinking, we've become overattached to computers whose software dictates what we'll produce on them, and even our bodies are increasingly the product of mechanistic interventions into them, from the programmed exercise routine to the implants that we will start to use to monitor our health – not to mention hearing-aids, pacemakers, and so on. And so, if the age of humanism, overlapping roughly with the Renaissance, marked the celebration by man of his own intellectual and artistic dominion, his self-determinism and his ability, rather than being enslaved to feudal lord or divine despot, to own himself and his actions, then the post-human age, by evolving cyborgian characteristics in us, reverses those advances. As such, it represents the fourth in the series of blows to human pride once listed, as it happens, by Freud. The first was the discovery by Copernicus that the earth goes round the sun, implying that mankind did not, and never had, sat at the centre of the universe; the second, Darwin's evidence that, rather than being God's special creatures, men derived from monkeys; and the third, Freud's own insight that man was displaced from himself by himself, riven by an unconscious that ate into his self-possession. You sleepwalk at night? Bah! You sleepwalk by day too.

I began this chapter by describing the humanity of sleep and have arrived at the post-human. But when the sleepwalker is guided back into bed, the humanity returns. It's a humanity which in this case, however, is not to do with defencelessness, amoral innocence or even mortality. Sleepwalking only exaggerates the strangeness of sleep – the being apart from one's conscious self. Your night-time journey is one in which you lose yourself for a while, before meeting up again in the morning. Being human involves an interlude, which we call sleep, between being yourself and being yourself again.

Afterword

BREAKFAST WITH SOCRATES is over, and you ask for the bill. It's been quite a conversation, and he's encouraged you to look at everything around you with a questioning eye. As the waiter comes towards your table, you might think back to Bert Hellinger's advice on letting your folks pay for lunch, for example, and consider how we return the favour to our parents for bringing us up, by taking care of their grandchildren. Or you might be tempted to do some investigating of your own: a little bit of research will turn up Jean-Paul Sartre's analysis of waiters:

> Let us consider this waiter in the café. His movement is quick and forward, a little too precise, a little too rapid. He comes towards the patrons with a step a little too quick [...] his voice, his eyes express an interest a little too solicitous for the order of the customer.

Sartre's tone verges on mockery: by hamming up the role rather than being himself, the waiter has compromised his own freedom. In a very waiterish way, he puts the bill on your table, and his performance makes you want to stop him and ask who he thinks he's kidding. Why can't he be less the waiter, and more the man?

And as you say goodbye to Socrates and head off to work, you might take comfort from now knowing that, although he might have got you to revise some of your most basic assumptions, you have an identity that will be cemented by the simple fact of leaving the café and arriving safely at the office. Or that, just by having got dressed, you've proven your ability to adapt to society. And even if having breakfast with Socrates has meant missing your morning workout at the gym, you've at least worked on your mind; besides, if Bakhtin and Foucault are right, gym-going only plays into the hands of those who want to control you.

But there's one last thing you might want to think about. Saying goodbye, like saying hello, is something so everyday that we rarely consider what's involved. As with the Spanish 'adios' ('to God') and the French 'adieu' (also 'to God'), the English 'goodbye' ('God be with you') commends the other person into the hands of the Lord for protection. As if you're saying 'Neither of us knows what's going to happen after we separate, but whatever it is, I hope God will take care of you', it's a recognition of the uncertainties that lie ahead, and of being vulnerable to them. Even when you take God out of the equation, saying goodbye involves more than valediction. The Italians and the Germans don't say goodbye but 'until I see you again'; both Arabic and Hebrew simply wish the other person peace; and even the apparently neutral 'farewell' expresses a clear hope for the other's wellbeing. Throughout all these phrases, what's obvious is that we never say goodbye when we say goodbye – we say something about the future. Indeed, for Jacques Derrida in his book *Adieu* – a homage to his late friend and fellow philosopher, Emmanuel Levinas – saying goodbye is far less about what's passed than what's to come.

Better therefore to think of a goodbye as a hinge that both closes down a period that's passed and known, and opens out to one still to be seen. There's a Swedish proverb that says, 'the afternoon knows what the morning never suspected', and if you say goodbye to someone after breakfast, you might each turn towards your day with a sense that there's something still undecided ahead of you, no matter how many appointments you have in your diary. And of course, one of the most unknown things of all is whether you'll ever see again the person you've just said goodbye to, and so the moment of parting always carries a certain pathos – every time we say goodbye could always be the last time, to combine songs by Ella Fitzgerald and the Rolling Stones.

And yet, despite that open-endedness, there's no getting round the fact that saying goodbye brings with it the sense of an ending, and, even as you read these lines, you'll have that unmistakeable sensation, sometimes comforting, sometimes saddening, that things are drawing to a close. As Samuel Beckett, albeit mischievously, says, 'all's well that ends'. The effort you've put into reading this book will be rewarded with a rounding-off which suggests that, for now at least, there's no more work to do. You'll make the transition from reading it to having read it, and being able to file it away both literally, on your bookshelf, and metaphorically, in the possibly more chaotic library of your mind where the books you've read are only partially recalled, some authors' names are rubbed out, and the ideas contained within them have got tangled up with episodes in your life. In both cases, the book recedes from this temporary prominence it has for you as you hold it, to take its place among the many other artifacts that over the years have contributed to your daily life.

Further reading

Philosophy

Jacques Derrida, *Points...: Interviews 1976–1993* (Stanford University Press, 1995)

René Descartes, *Discourse on Method and the Meditations* (Penguin, 2007)

Allan Janick and Stephen Toulmin, *Wittgenstein's Vienna* (Simon and Schuster, 1973)

Friedrich Nietzsche, *The Basic Writings of Nietzsche* (Random House, 2001)

Plato, *The Last Days of Socrates* (Penguin, 2003)

Psychoanalysis and Psychology

Sigmund Freud *The Interpretation of Dreams* (Penguin Freud Library, 1991); also *The Psychopathology of Everyday Life*, in the same series

Bert Hellinger, *Love's Hidden Symmetry: What Makes Love Work in Relationships* (Zeig, Tucker & Co, 1998)

Carl Jung, *Memories, Dreams, Reflections* (Flamingo, 1995)

Politics and Society

Walter Benjamin, *Illuminations* (Schocken Books, 1968)

Niccolo Machiavelli, *The Prince* (Penguin, 2004)

Karl Marx, *Capital: An Abridged Edition* (Oxford, 2008)

Carl Schmitt, *The Concept of the Political* (University of Chicago Press, 1996)

Max Weber, *From Max Weber* (Routledge, 1991)

Sociology and cultural studies

Jean Baudrillard, *Selected Writings*, 2nd edition (Polity, 2001)

Pierre Bourdieu, *Distinction: A Social Critique of the Judgement of Taste* (Routledge, 1986)

Claude Lévi-Strauss, *The Raw and the Cooked: Introduction to a Science of Mythology* (Pimlico, 1995)

Michel Foucault, *The Foucault Reader: An Introduction to Foucault's Thought* (Penguin, 1991)

Literature and literary theory

Roland Barthes, *A Roland Barthes Reader* (Vintage, 1993)

Andrew Bennett and Nicholas Royle, *An Introduction to Literature, Criticism and Theory: Key Critical Concepts* (Prentice Hall/Harvester Wheatsheaf, 1995)

Marcel Proust, *In Search of Lost Time* (Penguin, 2003)

Jean-Paul Sartre, *Nausea* (Penguin, 1963)

Index

A

Ackroyd, Peter, 111–12
Adam (Biblical figure), 17–18
Adorno, Theodor, 160
AIDS, 50
Albee, Edward: *Who's Afraid of Virginia Woolf?* (play and film), 147–52, 155
Allen, Woody, 145
Anaximander, 105
anima mundi see world-soul
animals: as food, 134–5
anomie (alienation), 68
anorexia nervosa, 58–9
Antony, Mark, 14–15, 21–2
apes: aquatic, 105–6
Archimedes, 104–5
arguing, 147–56
Aristophanes, 158–60
Aristotle, 66–7, 142
Auden, W. H.: 'Lullaby' (poem), 166–7
Augustine, St: *Confessions*, 108
authority, 30, 40
  doctors', 44–6, 51–2

B

Bach, Johann Sebastian, 106
Bacon, Francis, 1
Bakhtin, Mikhail, 99, 178
Barthes, Roland, 116–17
Bataille, Georges: *Story of the Eye*, 164–5
baths
  instructions for taking, 100–1
  nature of, 102–5
Baudelaire, Charles, 79
Baudrillard, Jean, 87
Beauvoir, Simone de, 104
Becket, St Thomas, 85
Beckett, Samuel, 179
Beethoven, Ludwig van: *Grosse Fugue in B flat major*, 132
being, 93–6
Benjamin, Walter, 79, 86
Beowulf (verse epic), 128–30
betrayal, 138

Bewick Thomas: *History of British Birds*, 112

Bhutto, Benazir, 110–11

Bible, Holy, 115–16

Blake, William: 'The Sick Rose' (poem), 47–8, 50

Blanchot, Maurice, 44

bodies
  and being, 93–6
  as 'carnival', 99
  and exercise, 93–4
  and illness, 45–8
  and mind, 50–51
  shaping and changing, 96–7

books, 110–17

Bosch, Hieronymus, 99

Bourdieu, Pierre, 131–2

Brillat-Savarin, Anthelme, 131
  The Philosopher in the Kitchen, 136

Brontë, Charlotte: *Jane Eyre*, 112–13

Buddha and Buddhism, 2, 103, 135

Burckhardt, Jacob, 12

bureaucracy, 38–9

Burton, Richard, 148

Bush, George W., 153

C

Cabaret (film), 12

cannibalism, 133–4

Canterbury, 86

capital, 35–7

Carlyle, Mara: 'Alive' (song), 4

Carlyle, Thomas, 18

Carrey, Jim, 67

Carroll, Lewis: *Alice's Adventures in Wonderland*, 113

Cervantes Saavedra, Miguel: *Don Quixote*, 116

chance, 15–16, 23

chaos, 15–16

Chapman, Jake and Dinos (sculptors), 99

charisma, 37–8

Chaucer, Geoffrey: *The Canterbury Tales*, 85

children
  dependence on parents, 54–6, 60–62
  upbringing, 63

Chopin, Frédéric: 'Farewell Song', 106–7

Christianity: and resurrection, 8–10

cinema, 121, 126

Cixous, Hélène, 150

class (social)
  differences, 35, 39
  struggle, 42

cleanliness, 20–22

'Cleanness' (poem), 20

Cleopatra, 14, 17, 21–2

Coleridge, Samuel Taylor, 84

collective unconscious, 173

Comfort, Alex: *The Joy of Sex*, 161–2, 164
commuting (travel), 24–5, 28, 30–31
Conrad, Peter, 119
conscience, 93–4
consciousness, 5–7, 9–10, 13
  see also unconscious, the
Constellations, 57–8
Cook, His Wife and Her Lover, The (film), 3, 133–4
cooking, 129–30, 136
Copernicus, Nicolaus, 8, 176
crowds, 28–9

D
Darwin, Charles, 160, 176
death, 8–9
  inevitability, 96
Deleuze, Gilles, 120
Derrida, Jacques, 28, 71, 88
  Adieu, 178
  The Post Card, 88
Descartes, René, 5–6, 8
dialectic, 11
Dickens, Charles, 111–12
doctors
  authority, 44–6, 51–2
  jokes about, 43–4
doubt, 5, 7–8
dreams, 169–42
dress (clothing), 17–19
Dubai, 73–4
Durkheim, Émile, 67–70

E
eating, 129–30
  see also food
Echo (mythological figure), 78
economic growth, 13
ecstasy, 163
ego, the (the 'I'), 19–20, 170
  see also superego
Eliot, T. S., 24
Emerson, Ralph Waldo, 90, 117
Emoto, Masaru: *The Message from Water*, 106
Eucharist, 56
Eve (Biblical figure), 17–18
exercise (physical), 91–3
existence: awareness of, 5–6

F
families: relationships and constellations, 57–8
fantasising, 25, 32
Fassbinder, Reiner Werner, 121
feminism, 150–51
fish: as food, 136–7
Fitzgerald, Ella, 179
'flâneurs', 79
Fleming, Sir Alexander, 52
food
  and child-parent relationship, 54–6, 58–61
  decay and maturation, 130–32
  and population levels, 59–60
  prohibitions and taboos, 131
  raw and cooked, 129–30, 132

and sacrifice, 57
Fosse, Bob, 12
Foucault, Michel, 2, 42, 98, 178
   History of Sexuality, 165
France: feminism in, 150–51
Frankfurt School of social
   theory, 160
free will, 16–17, 22
freedom
   and ideal of happiness, 66,
     69–70
   of individual, 63–6, 68–9
Freud, Sigmund
   on child play, 71
   on delayed effect, 77
   on sublimation, 19
   and the unconscious, 170,
     176
   The Interpretation of Dreams,
     168–70, 172–4
friendship, 142–4, 161

G

García Márquez, Gabriel *see*
   Márquez, Gabriel García
Gnosticism, 51
God
   and holidays, 84–5
   and subjection of chaos, 16
   and valedictions, 178
Godfather, The (film), 141
goodbyes, 178–9
Gore, Lesley, 138
Greenaway, Peter, 3, 134

Grendel (epic monster), 128–30
Guinness Book of Records, 113
gymnasiums, 91–3, 97–9

H

Haigh, John George, 102
happiness: as ideal, 66, 69
Hardy, Thomas: *Jude the
   Obscure*, 58
harm principle, 64–6
heavy metal (music), 106
Hegel, Georg Wilhelm
   Friedrich
   on absolute truth, 11–12
   curiosity, 1
   and dialectic, 11
   on history, 11–12
   on masters and slaves, 36
Heidegger, Martin, 94, 96
Heisenberg, Werner Karl:
   uncertainty principle, 15
Hellinger, Bert, 57, 62, 177
hermeneutics, 115, 117
Herzog, Werner, 121
Hinduism, 135
history
   Hegel on, 11–12
   Marx on, 12, 36
   and narrative, 111–12
Hitchcock, Alfred, 102
Hitler, Adolf, 134–5
Hobbes, Thomas: on crowds
   and daily commute, 3, 29–30
holidays, 82–4, 86–90

I

I, the *see* ego, the
ideal, the: and the real, 25–6
identity (selfhood), 26–9
Illich, Ivan, 45
illness
    bodily, 45–8
    and cures, 51–2
    as metaphor, 49–50
images, 124–5
Irigaray, Luce, 150
Islam
    and awakening, 9
    and pilgrimage to Mecca, 85

J

Jaques, Elliott, 39–40
Jaws (film), 129
Jerusalem: Wailing Wall, 85
Jesus Christ
    Jewish and Islamic
      interpretation of, 116
    resurrection, 8, 11
    and Stations of the Cross, 85
jobs *see* work
John of the Cross, St, 85
Jones, Quincy: 'It's My Party'
    (song), 138
Jung, Carl Gustav, 173–4

K

Kama Sutra, 161
Kant, Immanuel
    on dogmatic slumbers, 12

    on perception and pure
      reason, 7–8
Kellogg, Will Keith, 68
Kristeva, Julia, 150–51

L

labour
    for money, 33–5, 37
    see also work
Lacan, Jacques, 2, 77–8
language
    impurities in, 128
    and meaning, 108–10
Larkin, Philip, 60
Las Vegas, 87–8
leadership, 37–8
Lévi-Strauss, Claude: *The Raw
    and the Cooked*, 129–31, 134
Levinas, Emmanuel, 178
love, 138–9, 143, 149
    and sex, 160–61, 163–4
Lucretius: 'On the Nature of
    Things', 15

M

McCarthy, Cormac: *The Road*,
    134
Machiavelli, Niccolò, 2, 139–43,
    145
    The Prince, 141
McLuhan, Marshall, 123–4
Magaluf, Majorca, 87
malls (shopping), 73–6,
    78–80

Malthus, Thomas, 57, 59–60
manufacturing economy, 41
markets (trading), 74–6
Márquez, Gabriel García: *One Hundred Years of Solitude*, 112–13, 115, 117–18
Marx, Karl
  on history, 12, 36, 42
  on labour, 33–4, 37
  on rich and poor, 36, 39
  on wage slavery, 2
Maslow, Abraham, 55
medicine, alternative, 50–51
meditation, 103
Mill, John Stuart: on individual freedom, 63–7, 69
Milton, John: *Paradise Lost*, 17
Miró, Joán, 79
Mitterrand, François, 133
Monet, Claude, 79
Montaigne, Michel Eyquem de, 139, 143, 145
Monty Python (TV programme), 43
Morgan, Elaine, 105

N

Nabokov, Vladimir: *Lolita*, 110–11
Narcissus (mythological figure), 77–9
Nietzsche, Friedrich, 25–6, 28, 170

O

Obama, Barack, 153
obsession, 20
Ockham's razor, 22
optimism, 22
Orwell, George: *Nineteen Eighty-Four*, 124
Ovid, 77–8
  Ars Amatoria, 162

P

paganism: and occult, 10
pain, 45–6
parents: nourishing and care of young, 54–6, 60–62
Parker, Sarah Jessica, 122
parties and party-going, 138–46
philosophy: and question of consciousness, 5
pilgrimages, 85–6
Piranesi, Giovanni Battista, 88
placebos, 52–3
places: aura, 86–7
Plato
  on Socrates, 1
  on words, 108
  Symposium, 158
play: purpose of, 71
Ponge, Francis: *Soap*, 21–2
population levels, 59–60
Post-Traumatic Stress Disorder, 172
preparation (for action), 14–19, 22–3

Protestantism: and work ethic,
13, 37
Proust, Marcel: *In Search of Lost
Time*, 89, 112
psyche, 171
psychoanalysis, 173

R

reading, 112–16
reason, pure (Kantian), 7
Reception Theory, 113–15
resurrection, 8–10
Return of Martin Guerre, The
(film), 27
rhetoric, 152–4
ritual, 20
Rolling Stones (group), 179
Rothschild, Nathan Meyer, 1st
Baron, 35
routine, 20
running, 95
Rushdie, Salman: *The Satanic
Verses*, 115–16

S

Said, Edward, 132
Santiago de Compostela, 86
Sartre, Jean-Paul, 104, 177
Saussure, Ferdinand de, 110
Scarry, Elaine: *The Body in Pain*,
45
Schmitt, Carl, 2, 156
Schrödinger, Erwin, 113
Scott, Charles Prestwich, 119

Seinfeld (TV programme),
63
Self, 174
service economy, 41
sex
and love, 160–61, 163–4
manuals, 161–2, 164
as pleasure, 159–60
purpose of, 159–60
religious associations, 163
and seeing, 164–5
urge for, 157–9
Sex and the City (TV
programme), 122–3
sexuality: and dress, 18–19
Shadow, the, 174
Shakespeare, William
depicts Cleopatra, 14, 17
on sleep, 9
King Lear, 155
Sheldrake, Rupert, 106
Shelley, Percy Bysshe: on
carnivores, 134
shopping, 75–8, 80
showers, 101–2
Silence of the Lambs, The (film),
134
sin, 21
sleep, 166–7, 174–5
see also dreams
sleepwalking, 175–6
Socrates
curiosity, 1–2
death, 1

ideas, 177–8

Sontag, Susan: *Illness as Metaphor*, 48–50

Spencer, Stanley, 8–9

Spielberg, Steven, 102

Stevens, Wallace: 'Anecdote of the Jar' (poem), 74

structuralism, 130

suicide: and individual freedom, 68

superego, 19

Swift, Jonathan: *A Modest Proposal*, 59

T

taste, 131

Taylor, Elizabeth, 148

technological innovation, 13

Tel Quel (magazine), 150

television, 119–27

Teresa of Avila, St, 163

Thatcher, Margaret, Baroness, 41

time travel, 89

Truman Show, The (film), 67

truth

absolute (Hegelian), 11–12

paramountcy, 10–11

two worlds: doctrine of, 25

U

uncertainty principle, 15

unconscious, the, 170, 173–4

universal belief, 8

V

vegetarianism, 134–5

W

waiters, 177

waking up, 4–13

water

crystals, 106–7

neutrality, 107

Weber, Max

on capital, 36–7

on leadership, 37–8

on Protestant work ethic, 13

Welch, Jack, 37

Wenders, Wim, 121

wikiHow, 100, 104, 107

Wilde, Oscar, 145

William of Ockham, 22

Williams, Raymond, 122–3

Winkelmann, Eduard, 12

Winnicott, Donald, 70–71

wisdom, 2

Wittgenstein, Ludwig, 108–10

words, 108–11, 114

work

escape from, 63–71

nature of, 41–2

and office politics, 41

satisfaction with, 32–4

teams and hierarchies, 39–41

see also labour

work ethic, 13, 37

world-soul (*anima mundi*), 173–4